DO PARDON ME: TIPS FROM THE LIFE OF A DOCTOR WITH AUTISM

DO PARDON ME: TIPS FROM THE LIFE OF A DOCTOR WITH AUTISM

Dr Jonathan Yuen-Lee

Foreword by Professor Tony Attwood

First published in 2020

Copyright © 2020 by Jonathan Yuen-Lee

All rights reserved.

ISBN 9798615519239

No portion of this publication may be reproduced or transmitted in any form or by any means, mechanical or electronic, including photocopying, recording or by any information storage and retrieval mechanism, without prior written approval from the author. Requests to the author for permission and any correspondence should be addressed to JY188853@yahoo.com

Every possible effort has been made to fulfil obligations with regards to reproducing copyright material. The author will be pleased to rectify any omissions at the earliest opportunity.

Limit of liability/Disclaimer of Warranty: The author makes no representations or warranties with regards to the accuracy and completeness of the contents of this publication and specifically disclaim all warranties, including without limitation warranties of fitness for a particular purpose. The advice provided may not be suitable for every context. This publication is sold with the explicit understanding that the author is not engaged in rendering medical, legal and/or other professional advice. The author shall not be liable for damages arising herefrom. Reference to individuals, organizations or websites as citations and/or sources of additional information does not mean that the author endorses the information that the individuals, organization or website provided and any recommendations made.

DO PARDON ME: TIPS FROM THE LIFE OF A DOCTOR WITH AUTISM

QUICK START GUIDE

- Are you thinking about how to survive in school as a person with Autism? See Chapter 1.
- Friendships and relationships can be challenging for anyone. For hot tips on how to survive and thrive, see Chapter 2.
- The journey through medical school is daunting yet rewarding. Chapter 3 offers advice on precisely how you can do this.
- Starting a career as a junior doctor? Go to Chapter 4.
- You will eventually end up working as a Consultant or senior doctor. Chapter 5 talks about the highs and the lows as well as managing your own business.
- Interested in personal growth and transformation? Go to Chapters 6 and 7.
- Just want a focus on the strengths of Autism and which career to embark on? Refer to Chapter 8.

Quote

"Knowing others is intelligence; knowing yourself is true wisdom. Mastering others is strength; mastering yourself is true power."

Lao-tzu, an ancient Chinese philosopher and writer

A NOTE FROM THE AUTHOR

This book and any advice that it contains is based on the author's personal experiences of growing up as a neurodiverse individual, living and working on the Autism Spectrum. Despite having a background in Medicine, no content should be taken as medical advice in any shape or form. Any ideas and suggestions in this publication are not intended as such and the author shall not be liable or responsible for any loss or damage allegedly arising from any suggestion and information within this publication. Before following any advice provided here, you should consult with your doctor and/or therapist and/or counsellor. This book has also been written for adults. If you are under 18, you should consult with your parents with regards to any of the material and suggestions contained herein.

Contents

FOREWORD BY PROFESSOR TONY ATTWOOD 1
INTRODUCTION 4
Chapter One 9
Chapter Two 47
Chapter Three 62
Chapter Four 96
Chapter Five 117
Chapter Six 155
Chapter Seven 171
Chapter Eight 203
Conclusion and Dedication 224
References 226
Further reading (includes the perspective of employers and colleagues) 229
INDEX 231

FOREWORD BY PROFESSOR TONY ATTWOOD

"A person with autism becoming a doctor, impossible!" could be the public's reaction to someone who has autism seeking a career in medicine. Autism is often perceived as a disability with significant deficits in social communication and interaction - essential qualities for a doctor. However, my extensive clinical experience leads me to believe that medicine can indeed be a wise career choice for those who have autism, and this includes all medical specialties, from pathology to psychiatry. It is important to recognise that the characteristics of autism can and do change over time, such that the person may acquire the abilities to engage in a reciprocal conversation and interaction, read nonverbal communication, and develop meaningful friendships and relationships. During the adult years, the signs of autism in a social interaction can become very subtle.

Many of the qualities and characteristics required for a person to become a doctor are those I have frequently found to be associated with autism: compassion; empathy; commitment; respect; an encyclopedic memory, along with the ability to accumulate and recall information; an ability to detect patterns and analyze systems. There is also a strong sense of social justice, and a determination to help those people who face health challenges in their daily lives.

We recognise that there is a high level of inheritance of the characteristics of autism. Recent research has explored this in relation to parental – particularly father's - occupations and established that highly systemizing occupations such as engineering, accountancy and medicine are associated with a greater propensity to have a child with autism (Dickerson et al 2014). The odds of having a child with autism are twice as high as the general population for fathers who are engineers, five times more likely for accountants, but seven times more likely if the father works in health care.

While some of the characteristics of autism can enable a successful medical career, there are, at the same time, characteristics of both autism and medicine that can cause considerable stress. These can include aspects of working in a team with complex social dynamics, the tendency for the person to be very self-critical, and their sensory sensitivity. There is also an association between autism and anxiety and depression: the high anxiety levels created by a job that is very responsible and frequently stressful can lead to an emotional and energy 'implosion', or breakdown. This is what happened to Jonathan.

I was aware of Jonathan's high reputation as a child and adolescent psychiatrist, and first met him after his breakdown. He is determined that fellow doctors, in training and qualified, learn from his experiences to ensure they manage their many sources of stress. His advice is wise, and I highly recommend *"Do Pardon Me"* for medical students and practitioners.

Professor Tony Attwood

INTRODUCTION

Hello there! Welcome, welcome. My name is Jonathan and it is a great honour and privilege to invite you to read my book. It is a Saturday today. Of all things, I have to say that I have just finished baking a gluten-free almond and orange cake and thought that this would be the best time to complete my introductory chapter. I was born in Malaysia. I worked for many years as a doctor and have several postgraduate qualifications after my name….. but above all else, I am a fellow human being. I hope to be able to share with you my life experience, the highs, the deepest depths of despair, the lessons learnt and the determination to keep going.

You may also be interested to know that I have been diagnosed with Autism. Indeed, a specific type on the spectrum that was known as Asperger's Syndrome. This does not necessarily mean that I am a super smart 'Aspie', socially awkward, perhaps geeky, nerdy, eccentric, weird or even alien. It means that I have a collection of signs and symptoms which fit into a diagnostic label classified as a disability. Unfortunately, through this label (which by the way implies mostly deficits rather than strengths), people may know a bit about who I am and a lot more about what I cannot do. I hope that through this book I will be able to change that. For this reason, I will avoid using the term disorder. Instead of Autism Spectrum Disorder, I will simply write Autism. I will refer to people with Autism as being neurodiverse, and people without Autism as being neurotypical.

It may be a surprise for you to learn that doctors can have Autism. Surely not? Is medicine not a socially and intellectually demanding profession? How can one survive as a doctor with Autism? Indeed, we are vulnerable too. The number of people with Autism in the world is increasing day by day for several reasons. Recent statistics show that we are facing an epidemic of Autism. As the younger generation grows older, more and more children with Autism will inevitably become adults with Autism who enter employment.

There are doctors who have personally experienced epilepsy, cancer, heart disease and diabetes. There are many in the helping professions who live with depression and anxiety. It is time to learn about the experience of people with Autism who work in the helping professions such as Medicine, Nursing, Dentistry, Pharmacy, Psychology, Social Work, Research, Teaching and so on. What is perhaps even more interesting is the high likelihood that there are many undiagnosed individuals already working successfully in those professions and others including Engineering, Computer Science, Animal Science, Music, Drama and Accountancy.

The process of writing this book has not been easy. Just a year ago, I could not have imagined this undertaking. Following a highly successful career, I had a major mental breakdown. I tasted vulnerability, loss and mental illness. I could have withdrawn under the covers refusing to see the light of day. I could have completed suicide. Instead, I chose a clean start by embarking on a new career path while using my skills as a doctor with Autism to continue helping others.

My story illuminates several important issues:

- Autism in Medicine as an emerging frontier in employment
- Gender and Autism where mimicry and camouflage are no longer gender exclusive

- Survival in Autism: when life events beyond our control and understanding occur. How we rise above them is what counts
- Autism and the Eastern philosophical dimension
- The importance of altruism and service to others for self-identity
- Transformation as a continual process of letting go: we need to release the old to bring in the new
- Replacing judgement with curiosity and compassion.

Each chapter is devoted to a specific part of my life which I hope will be of use to you in providing a context for these issues. I have written this book as a survival guide with hot tips at the end of each chapter. This book is for doctors and anyone in the helping professions who may have Autism or possess traits of Autism, including what was known as Asperger's Syndrome and Asperger traits. Some of the tips are repeated between chapters so it is fine to focus on a particular chapter relevant to your particular life stage. Whether you are just curious; an aspiring high school or university student; a working professional or simply know someone with Autism, I trust that the following pages will be of benefit by providing you with an alternative way of thinking about Autism and how it can be used as a gift to help others.

Chapter One
Fans, Toilets, Spaceships, A Cat and Music

Have you ever heard of a place called Kuching before? Well, it is a city in an Eastern state of Malaysia called Sarawak. It is next to an oil rich country called Brunei and is also located on the island of Borneo, the third largest island in the world. You may have heard of the Borneo Tropical Rainforests, the Mulu Caves and perhaps the (now extinct) head-hunters. Kuching comes from the Malay word Kucing which means cat. It is a rather strange coincidence, but a cat was my best friend as a child and perhaps fate would have it that I was born in the Cat City.

Malaysia is a multi-ethnic country and both my parents were Chinese folks who were also born in Sarawak. My great-grandparents came from mainland China. The Chinese dialect that I was raised with was based on the parts of China that my great-grandparents grew up in. My father was Hokkien. You may have heard of Hokkien noodles. My mother was Cantonese which is the first language of many Hong Kong Chinese Restaurants. Despite these dialects, I was actually raised with English and Malay as my first languages.

Malaysia is still a developing (third world) country. When I was born, Kuching was a town and only achieved city status many years later. It is now a bustling city with an international airport, several universities, hospitals and a significant tourism industry. These places that many of us take for granted in developed nations were only things to be dreamed of in my childhood.

My parents, Simon and Jacinta met at a Beauty Pageant. My father was having time off work as an Engineer and went with several of his friends to the local pageant where he was apparently captivated by my mother who was the winner of the day! And so, the story goes with my father courting my mother and their marriage the following year.

I am one of two children. I was born into this world three years before my sister Helena. My mother recently shared with me her experience of having me. As much as I was loved and wanted, she had to endure severe morning sickness in the first three months. I was born at term naturally in our town hospital following a 12-hour labour. This was longer than usual and my father was not present as per local hospital policy at the time.

Apparently, I ate and slept well as an infant. My earliest memories were of a bouncing net which was used to help me fall asleep before I was moved into a cot. I remember the cloth like material used for the bouncing net. Persons with Autism can have very vivid visual childhood memories. I certainly recall being bounced up and down and also remember quite clearly my mother being pregnant with Helena as she lay in bed with a big tummy.

The first 6 weeks of my life were known as the Chinese "confinement period". This is a traditional practice in our culture. My grandmother, Mary explained that she would wrap me up tightly in a blanket for comfort. My hands were also tied with ribbons as was cultural practice at the time. I have since wondered how appropriate this would be considered today and what impact it had on my sensory development on the Autism spectrum. Deep pressure continues to have a calming effect on me. Back and foot massages as well as wrapping myself up tightly with a blanket during sleep has certainly been helpful for stress and anxiety.

My mum and dad describe me as a somewhat serious and quiet infant who did not spontaneously seek physical affection. I was not the touchy, feely and cuddly type. Nevertheless, I could still smile, giggle and cackle in response so was not quite the robot baby. Eye contact was not consistent. This was not considered out of the normal range at the time. I do recall frequent comments from my teachers and schoolmates about needing to lighten up and not appear so serious most of the time. No one knew that this was not simply a personality or character trait but subtle signs of Autism.

Another important figure in my life was the family maid whom we referred to as "Kakak" which in Malay means big sister. Maids are part of the family structure in many parts of Asia where it is considered the norm and a cost-effective way of obtaining home help in return for food and lodging. Many maids hailed from the longhouse villages out of town or from neighbouring Indonesia. For a small amount of money at the time, maids were in charge of looking after the children while the parents went to work, shopping, cooking and just about everything around the home. We had several maids over the years, but I have the most vivid memories of Raya and Jenny.

Raya Kakak was a fabulous cook. She came to my rescue when a huge caterpillar dropped from the tree onto my head in the garden one day. Jenny Kakak I will always remember as the poor maid who woke up one night with a snake hissing by her bedside. We had just moved into a new family home which was next to a forest plantation. Snakes were certainly not uncommon, and Jenny woke up screaming one night when a snake had crawled through the drain pipes into her bedroom. As I grew older, maids became less affordable and we no longer had the privilege of maids by the time I was in my mid-primary years. Having a "big sister" around the home was a big plus in my earlier childhood and certainly cushioned feelings of isolation and loneliness.

I was introduced to the rituals and practices of the Roman Catholic Church very early on. I can still visualise my Baptism ceremony with the pouring of Holy Water in the presence of my Godfather Mr Chee who was also an Engineer like my father. Catholic rituals played a significant part in my early childhood. This included attending Mass weekly to receive Communion, saying grace before meals and going to Confession at least twice a year.

I am quite certain that this early exposure to religious rituals which provided a predictable form of comfort also played an essential role in the development of several Obsessive-Compulsive behaviours. I later learnt during my medical training that compulsions in the context of an Obsessive-Compulsive Disorder are quite different to other forms of compulsive behaviour. Instead of providing comfort, they are a source of distress and anxiety. They need to be performed to alleviate any associated discomfort. For me, I simply had to pray a certain number of times repeatedly until it felt just right, or I had reached the magic number in my head. Otherwise, I suffered terribly from irrational fears that some catastrophe would befall myself or my family. Beliefs and rituals also played an essential role in an Autistic childhood as was the case for me since my pre-primary and early primary school years. These rituals came in many shapes and forms. Beliefs are what a child thinks, and rituals refer to the specific behaviours which are much more easily observed by others.

Religiosity in Autism can thus be viewed as a constellation of behaviours that the Autistic child finds soothing to perform and as a way of understanding the ununderstandable. It is when these behaviours become distressing for the individual child that ongoing exposure to religious practices need to be carefully managed and the child's spiritual needs nourished in a less ritualistic manner. It is unlikely that the Autistic child will be able to make the distinction between what is soothing and what is compulsive, so it will be up to the parents and close family members to be aware and set appropriate limits to ritualistic behaviours. God the Father, Jesus and the Holy Spirit provided a framework in which I could process anything that I did not understand. As an Autistic visual thinker, it was particularly important for me to see and not just hear. The images from prayer books of Jesus and his mother Mary would be forever ingrained in my memory. While the rituals became a source of distress, the images remained a source of comfort into my adulthood.

I walked and talked early. I was able to speak in single words and sentences before one year. Most people perceive Autism as a condition in which an individual is not able to speak. This is not true. There are those on the spectrum who can speak very well, often using big words and a formal style of speaking from an early age. They can establish eye contact and do not flap their hands, contrary to the stereotype of Autism.

My father, Simon was trained as a Civil Engineer. For the first two years of my life, he frequently worked away visiting various engineering sites, road works and water plants across the state of Sarawak. For this reason, my mother, grandmother, maids and uncles were my main carers and role models. I recall being very excited whenever my father returned home from his travels. He would pull up in a big government car after being picked up at the airport.

My paternal grandmother, Mary, whom I call Mama, continues to be a big part of my life. Autism is not part of her vocabulary so we as a family have struggled to explain to her that I have a particular "condition" that makes it more difficult for me to develop relationships with other people. Nevertheless, my main memories of her are of playing card games, clearing the wax out of my ears, completing jigsaw puzzles, making dumplings for my noodles and going to her home for sleepovers with my rattan weaved suitcase.

My maternal uncles were also a great influence in my earlier life. I suppose they filled in the gap for my father. My mother, Jacinta was born and raised in regional Sarawak. She lived on a farm with her parents and 7 siblings. She has 6 brothers. As the final years of high school were not offered in their local high school, four of my uncles came to live with us in Kuching to complete their pre-university studies. All these uncles were essentially my best buddies. They helped me with my studies, homework and taught me how to play badminton, a very Asian sport.

Uncle Albert, who is now an Engineer, helped me build my confidence in English. Uncle Chris was the quietest of the lot. He is now a Mechanical Engineer. Uncle Peter was helpful and playful. He is now an Orthodontist. Uncle Isaac who did not actually live with us strongly encouraged me to study medicine being a doctor himself. He later went on to become a very talented Urologist which in hindsight is an interesting connection to my fascination with toilets and my father's later work as a Water Supply and Sewerage Engineer.

It was sad for me to see my uncles leave for university, but I was fortunate enough to have one uncle replaced by the other. To this day, even though I did not appreciate them early on as much as I should have, I am greatly honoured to have known these men and for the influence they had on me in my childhood years.

Male role models are crucial in a boy's development. I must emphasise the importance of neurotypical male role models for an Autistic boy who needs to learn by mirroring and observation of others. It is quite possible that if you have Autism, your father has similar traits, so it would be crucial to engage with other positive male influences to help develop how you interact and communicate with people.

I have come to understand and accept that obsessions in Autism come and go with one replaced by another. My obsession with cars arose from the big office cars that my father travelled in for work. My father's first car was a white Mazda Capella with a manual transmission. My earliest memories of this car were the difficulties it had pulling up the hill on the way to church. There were several times when I thought the car was not going to make it! There was only one public park in Kuching named the Reservoir Park. I went there to play on the swings and ride on the seesaws with my grandmother. The exit from the carpark had a particularly steep incline. There were several occasions when the car stalled midway and indeed even rolled backwards once! Fortunately, the car behind us quickly reversed out of the way. Perhaps they heard us screaming. We subsequently used my parents second car, an Opel Manta which had a stronger 1.8L engine to cope with the incline.

Opel Manta

The Opel Manta holds a special place in my car memories. It was a two-door coupe engineered in Germany and sold to my father in 1972 for a significant sum of $14,000 (Malaysian ringgit). It exuded much style with its pillarless windows, chrome bumper trim and curvaceous top. It bore a resemblance to the classic Batmobile with its tail fins and characteristic exhaust note. We could not afford to have an air conditioner installed at the time and had to make do with the factory installed hot air blower. It tended to overheat in traffic as the radiator system was clearly not designed for the hot and humid Malaysian weather.

I became quite obsessed with car radiator fans. It was not just their spinning nature but the range of sounds they produced. At the time, the best sounding car fan was of a Volvo 240GL. I could only describe it as a distinct roar and always raced out of the house if there was one that came into the neighbourhood.

My parents third car was a 1981 Honda Accord which came with two electric radiator fans. As a child, I would sit ahead of the front grille to enjoy the sound of these fans and the movement of air through my fingers into the engine bay. I discovered later on that I could take the fans out of the radiator, plug them to a standalone car battery and watch them spin for an in-home soothing effect. I became so immersed in car radiator fans that I included the installation of a secondary electric radiator fan for the Opel Manta to supplement the fan belt driven main fan as a reward for doing well in my school examinations.

The obsession with car fans evolved into an obsession with car cleaning. My father had an office driver whom we nicknamed "The Dog" in a nice way because he was talented in many things and was able to eat any kind of food, or so I was told. He cleaned the office car, which was a Toyota Cressida at least daily and this was no mean feat given the wet tropical weather. He taught me to roll down the windscreens to clean the upper edges as well as the best way to clean the wiper blades with a pair of tissues. Cleaning cars was therapeutic in many ways, but it also became a compulsion as I developed an irresistible urge to clean the car each time it had been on the roads or whenever there was a smear on the windscreen.

I was quite sickly as a child and experienced recurrent fevers with tonsillitis and sinusitis. I was on regular antibiotics and painkillers. I appeared to have a high tolerance for pain and did not cry as much as expected. My detachment from physically and emotionally challenging experiences was probably another Autistic trait. I had a febrile convulsion lasting several minutes when just 12 months old. I vividly recall my mother inserting her thumb into my mouth to prevent self-injury. Headaches occurred at least once a week. In retrospect, these arose not only from the sinuses but also from my sensitivities to light and sound as well as an undiagnosed gluten intolerance. Asian noodles were a staple food and no one in the family knew that some of the foods I consumed would have a detrimental impact on my physical and emotional health. A family ritual was going to hawker stalls by the roadside for either Kuching Kolo Mee (a popular noodle dish) or Sarawak Laksa (vermicelli with shredded chicken in a spicy broth).

During my frequent doctor visits, I developed a curiosity towards the field of medicine and the notion of helping others. I had two GPs and an ENT surgeon whom we consulted. They prescribed a variety of bitter to sweet tasting medications directly from their practices as there were no separate pharmacies to dispense medications in Malaysia. In the end, I needed a tonsillectomy as the repeated infections were affecting my sleep and energy levels during the day. Uncle Isaac who was training as a Surgeon at the time accompanied me for the procedure. It was a very distressing time and I recall screaming into the operating theatre before the anaesthetist asked me to breathe into a fruit flavoured mask. This was my first ever recollection of a panic attack. Whilst my sinus symptoms and headaches improved after the operation, I distinctly recall the tone of my voice changing and my headaches still occurring, albeit on a less frequent basis.

In addition to seeing western doctors, I was seen by a range of Chinese Medicine Practitioners at the behest of my grandmother. Through observation of them, I learnt about the role of Chinese Medicine in the treatment of acute, and more significantly, chronic ailments. A Chinese Medicine doctor comes to a diagnosis by studying your pulse. Of course, there was no awareness of Autism at the time. I was prescribed a variety of Chinese medicines to strengthen my liver, lungs and kidneys. These did not taste great and I recall taking them because I had to rather than because I wanted to due to any benefits. In a similar vein, I had regular foot reflexology sessions which focussed on specific parts of my feet to improve the headaches and sinus pains. The most important impact of Chinese Medicine in my life was the discovery of life energy known as Qi and the practice of Tai Chi and Qi Gong. My grandmother and my mother practised this slow form of exercise regularly. It not only became a joint activity with them but also an appropriate sensory strategy to manage stress and anxiety. I will elaborate on these in a later chapter.

I was fascinated and then obsessed with toilets from an early age. I suppose this coincided with Sigmund Freud's teachings about the toilet training stage. I could not stop asking repeated questions about toilets such as the different types, how they worked and what would happen if they did not. I loved my potty. I flushed any toilets I could get my hands on repeatedly, opened the cisterns to check out the mechanisms and needed regular reminders not to use too much toilet paper and block the toilets. I was simply immersed with watching the flow of water into the cisterns and how a simple balloon mechanism could turn the water on and off. This fascination with toilets fluctuated over the years to come before I became obsessed with toilet humour as a means of socialising with others.

Unfortunately, I severely underestimated the impact that sound would have on my emotional wellbeing. It was clearly a cause of my headaches. A photograph of myself in Year 2 covering my ears with my hands while the rest of the class was dancing was later confirmed as a clear sign of Autism. Everything seemed very loud and close. I lost sense of how much was too little or too much. I was acutely sensitive to smells in any rooms that other people could not detect. There was no concept of what a sensory profile and sensory diet was during those days and it was a miracle that I managed to survive the sensory onslaught on my senses.

The most important sensory coping mechanism I developed on my own was to drown out all my senses to the sound of classical and pop music. I learnt the Piano for 8 years and came to know various music styles from various composers which were conducive to the Autistic mind. This included Beethoven and his symphonies, Elgar and his variations, Mozart and his concertos, Tchaikovsky's ballets and Cathedral Choir Music. Later, I developed an interest in musical theatre after an introduction by my form Teacher who lent me a musical cassette. The lyrics and music from Phantom of the Opera, Miss Saigon, the Sound of Music, Oliver and Les Misérables were ever present to help me cope with the schooling years. I immersed myself in a particular theatrical role within the confines of my bedroom or bathroom. I found that adopting a range of different personas from the musical characters helped me cope with the isolation and sadness of childhood. I amassed a collection LPs and Cassette tapes before the advent of CDs and internet audio.

I was fascinated with the English choral tradition and it is quite likely that the discipline associated with learning this form of music as a young boy helped me develop the perseverance that I needed to manage the social and sensory demands of early childhood and focus, perhaps too much, on my studies. There are many famous musicians on the Autism spectrum. I am sure that the study of music for those individuals was an important way to learn about how their autistic mind work, develop ways to cope and use their gifts to bring happiness to the lives of others.

In retrospect, I preferred to play on my own or with my own selected company of friends who were not my age. They were either older or younger than me. I did not share spontaneously. I was described as shy, modest or unassuming by most relatives and needed prompting to say hello and goodbye. In groups with other children, I would play at the periphery and be quite happy to do my own thing.

Friendships and relationships in Autism are the subjects of the next chapter.

I enjoyed building blocks and lining things up. Everything had to look symmetrical and just right. It was during this time that I came across Lego® which would later become an important part of my working life. Lego® was scarce in Malaysia at the time, so my father obtained my first Lego® set during his travels in Singapore. This was a spaceship which was released many years later as Benny's spaceship from the Lego® Movie. The set was built repeatedly, initially based on the instructions but as I grew more confident with my building skills, I modified it based on what I had seen from TV shows. Playing with this set was my first memory of using a toy in a semi imaginative way to pass my time.

Contrary to the perception that children with Autism do not have an imagination, I had a very active one centred around my special interests and obsessions. Science Fiction role-play, copied from my favourite series Battlestar Galactica, was an integral part of my childhood and another means of solitary play. I would use my hands to model various spacecraft and with the associated self-made sound effects would fly around the house at light speed attacking each other. For those of you who know the Cylons from the original Battlestar Galactica species, they spoke in a very appealing Autistic monotone.

Firecrackers were a big tradition during the Chinese New Year festive period, particularly on the first and the last or 15th day. The sound was meant to ward off evil spirits. Although the loud bang was too much for my senses, I was thrilled with lighting the fuse, running away and the reaction of others to the explosion. To promote safety, my father insisted that I light the fuse with a cigarette butt or joss stick tip tied to the end of a fishing rod. In this way, I came to learn that Autism comes with "sensory in the extremes". Many sensory experiences are aversive, but some can be very attractive, particularly if they are made by the child.

In my early primary school years, I attended a private coeducational school. I was "adored" by my teachers and popular amongst the girls who were probably attracted to my intelligent, sensitive and gentle nature. I had boys and girls as friends but was often teased by the boys for playing with the girls and wearing spectacles. I came home very upset one day and reported to my mother that a boy had rubbed his "dirty" shoes on my shirt. This was another sign of my obsession around cleanliness. Overall, girls were much more accepting and patient. My gentle nature, my observation and copying of their social mannerisms nurtured me into a gentlemanly manner which would be detrimental to me as I entered adolescence.

I developed other solitary activities which helped me cope with the perplexing social world at the time. I enjoyed reading Enid Blyton, Agatha Christie, writing in my diary, and collecting matchboxes from hotels and restaurants. I aimed to read every single series from Enid Blyton and looked forward to attending the Agatha Christie movie nights at the British Council Library. I have kept these diaries to this date. The entries were, not surprisingly, very repetitive and structured. My life was very predictable from sunrise to sunset, with a self-initiated schedule which consisted of waking up, eating breakfast, washing my face, brushing my teeth, going to school, doing my homework, attending extra classes, completing eye exercises to improve my short sightedness and saying prayers before bed. They did not speak at all about how I felt emotionally at the time of my childhood nor did they elaborate on any social interactions with other people that I had at the time.

Animals played a very important part of my childhood and this is particularly the case for anyone with Autism, diagnosed or otherwise. I had many dogs named Boxer, Buddy, Frisco, Disney, Spike and Jean Luc. Buddy was the most loyal but also the fiercest. Dogs were essential to growing up in Malaysia as we were prone to burglars from Kalimantan which is part of Indonesia on the island of Borneo. My parents recalled many terrifying stories of their friends being tied up at home or cast under a spell, so that they were completely paralysed while the thieves ransacked their homes.

My strongest emotional attachment during childhood was to my cat whom I named Meme. Meme was given to us by my neighbour, Georgia. She was a stray kitten whom they found near their home with the brightest blue eyes and a stub for a tail. I suspect Meme was a Manx crossed with a Siamese. We almost lost Meme when she first arrived into our home as Buddy, being the dog that he was, chased her into the neighbouring forest plantation. I think it was my father who managed to restrain her from crawling under the fence and slipping away. Buddy and Meme later became friends and they both lived long lives until I left Malaysia to pursue my studies.

I personally believe it is essential for any child with Autism to have a pet. I owe a great part of my childhood survival to Meme and only realised this in retrospect. She was there for me every day and whenever I was upset from feeling lonely. She was my constant companion when I studied for examinations. We seemed to have a school test at least every two weeks. There is a non-judgemental approach about animals that put me immediately at ease. I am quite sure that Meme was able to understand me and, in many ways, communicate with me non-verbally. She had a forceful and strong *meow* which varied in tone according to her emotional state.

Meme

I also reared fish for several years and developed an obsession with aquarium filters. I read the books I had about filters repeatedly and surveyed all the aquarium shops in Kuching for the different models and mechanisms. Just like my obsession with toilets, I was simply fascinated by the flow of water in filters. It was also an outlet for my compulsive cleaning tendencies. I probably had the shiniest aquarium in the neighbourhood. My main caution would be the aversive smell of the fish. I needed to use gloves to prevent contamination, a practice derived from my fear of germs. If you are sensitive to loss, rearing fish may not be a good idea due to their unpredictable life spans.

There were several neighbourhood children with whom I socially engaged. Most were the children of Teachers and Engineers like my parents. We connected through our pets, playing detective from the storybooks we had read, badminton over the fence (yes, another Asian activity) and tuition classes. School classes ran from 0710 to 1250. In the afternoons, I had the opportunity to complete homework or return to school for sports and various clubs. It was also traditional practice for parents to send children to extra tuition classes which would run in the afternoons, evenings and weekends.

I attended English classes which were enjoyable as they were 1:1 with a British tutor. I found the Malay language classes socially confronting and never engaged in any chit chat with my fellow classmates before or after the lessons. Surprisingly, I found the art classes on the weekends much more appealing. It was probably because they consisted of children from a range of age groups and ran on a weekend. I went with my sister and two neighbours who were younger than me. It was routine for us to walk to the Sunday classes.

During the times we walked back, we would see who could scream the loudest all the way home. I was quite good at art, particularly if it involved copying a scene or drawing objects. Drawing people, any form of social interaction and drawing from my imagination was virtually impossible.

My mother was the centre of my human universe. She was very devoted to me and nowadays one could describe the relationship in psychological terms as enmeshed. I depended on her as much as she depended on me. She was an extremely hard worker. I have hardly seen her sit still or relax. She was a good Maths, Science and English teacher who taught in both coeducational and single sex schools. She started off in high school before moving to primary school teaching prior to taking early retirement. To make ends meet and to fund my overseas studies, she gave tuition classes from home in the afternoon. Being a teacher, she probably spoke too loudly for the Autistic senses and gave one too many lectures to an obedient child. Complete respect for parents and the use of the cane for any misbehaviour was also the cultural norm of the time.

My father has always been a mystery to me. He was a very dutiful man, providing for us very honestly despite working in a culture that was prone to corruption. He called home whenever he was away and always brought us a gift upon returning. We looked forward to the special treats of Kentucky Fried Chicken (or their competitor Sugar Bun Chicken) when he returned home from work. In hindsight, my father has become more Autistic over time. I desperately craved his affection, approval and acceptance. As an adult, I spent more and more money on cars and travel to impress him. I have worked very hard to view him with an attitude of compassion and gratitude for all that he has done. Above all, I am grateful to still have a father, when many people I know have already lost theirs.

My sister was a completely different person from myself. She was probably more neurotypical than my parents or me. We had shared interests in the books that we read, the piano, and our love of Meme, but I always longed for a brother instead of or in addition to a sister. She was much more fiercely independent, outgoing and less compliant. She was not afraid to stamp her feet in retaliation to my parents. My father seemed to obsess over her and I gather she found this difficult to cope with.

Copying and mimicry is an important survival strategy in Autism. Who you are exposed to is so essential in determining your future sense of self. I discovered shortwave radio while at the home of my father's engineering friend. I was fascinated by the long wave, short wave and medium wave dials as well as the notion that you could listen to other countries from afar. As much as my father had the Voice of America on throughout the night, I tuned into the BBC and it was through this channel that I developed and refined an English accent. Listening to the world radio provided a means of connection with the outside world.

In Grades 4 and 5, I moved to a government coeducational school which was closer to home. I was always liked by my teachers. Comments in my report card included "responsible, dutiful and diligent student". Those were probably the happiest years of my life. I felt accepted by my peers and was appointed Class Prefect. I was almost always top of the class academically and referred to as "The Professor". I had long phone conversations after school with several girls and did not feel alone during those years. We spoke about TV series and what we did day to day. I used the opportunity to socially analyse the friendship dynamics in school.

For my last grade of primary school, I was moved to an all-boys school. I appeared less happy in this school but eventually made friends with several boys. Others thought that I was not "helpful, friendly and cooperative". Unfortunately, it was not seen as a sign of Autism, but rather snobbery and selfishness. I took daily public transport on a school bus for the first time. Although I took the bus with my neighbour who was three years my Senior, and a good Badminton friend, I did not like the unpredictability in its arrival times, especially when the roads were flooded with the heavy monsoon rains. Floods were very frequent in those days and we were fortunate to live on high ground. I really struggled with the queues and crowds. My intolerance of heat and humidity became more evident. During this time, I developed an obsession with air conditioners and how they worked. This is definitely connected to my preoccupation with the flow of water, air and fans. I was immediately thrilled when my bedroom window unit was replaced with a Toshiba split system air conditioner. It was very therapeutic watching the spinning fan and sitting inside in front of the cool blowing air.

I was voted Classroom Monitor in Grade 7, but my peers did not like my controlling style. I strictly followed the Teachers rules in a no-nonsense manner and was disappointingly outvoted the following year. I was teased very intensely and called many hurtful names. The emotional scars from bullying lasted much longer than any physical scars. I coped by taking regular toilet breaks from class and isolating myself further from my peers. Toilets became a sanctuary whenever I was away from home and feeling stressed. Surprisingly, the safety of toilets and the sound of running water overrode the potentially overwhelming smells one might expect in a school lavatory.

Several school friends were eccentric to say the least. I am sure that one of them who walked very clumsily and spoke like a robot was on the Autism spectrum. This small group always sat at the front of the class and were the top academic achievers. We were poor at team sports and refrained from play during classroom breaks. Unfortunately, I did not maintain contact with them after leaving school but their presence underscores the importance of having a group of likeminded friends in school that can serve as a shield to the social and sensory demands of that setting.

Individual sports were important for physical fitness. Badminton was an essential prosocial activity. I could play this over the fence or gate with my neighbours and it did not come with the stress of having to analyse the body language, motives and intentions of a group of people. I also found swimming an area of strength which bolstered my confidence. It also improved my core muscle strength and gross motor coordination skills. I was moderately successful at tennis. Sports that did not resonate with me included soccer, a Malaysian sport known as Sepak Takraw (which involved kicking or knocking a rattan ball over the net with one's head) and basketball.

My interest in commercial aeroplanes grew gradually toward the end of my primary school years. Like the different models of cars and vivid recollection of their license plate numbers, I learnt to recognise aeroplane models by sight. Kuching had a relatively small airport so the planes I grew up with consisted of Fokker 50s and 737s. My father shared this passion, and plane spotting became a cherished father-son activity for many years.

Tips (parents, families and educators take special note):

- The early signs of Autism are subtle, particularly for those on the higher functioning end of the spectrum. These include anxiety, perfectionism, social avoidance and sensory modulation difficulties, particularly to sound. It may be even less evident in Eastern cultures where the emphasis is on compliance and educational outcomes. It is crucial for adults around the child to be aware of these signs, adjust their approach towards discipline and set more appropriate expectations. It is not in the best interest of the child to expect that he or she will grow out of it.
- The choice of school is crucial. Although the mode of educational delivery and supports required will vary from child to child, since copying and mimicry is such an important survival mechanism, I would have preferred to remain in a coeducational setting for all my schooling years. This would have provided more balance to my development, shelter from the bullies, more acceptance and opportunities to develop relationships with girls.

- The relationship between siblings needs to be nurtured. It is highly likely that the neurotypical sibling will be considered as having a completely different personality and character. While this may be the case, any areas of joint interest need to be cultivated and numerous opportunities provided for the child with Autism to learn from the sibling by mirroring and observation. If the older child has Autistic tendencies, he or she should not be given sole responsibility of being a role model for the younger sibling.
- Stress, anxiety, perfectionism and the need to be in control should be actively addressed early on. While it is an appropriate strategy to face anxieties in order for them to get better, repeated exposure to sensory sensitivities is inappropriate and does not work.
- The desire to fit in is so high that the child with Autism is highly vulnerable to being bullied by other students AND adults. While the child needs to be explicitly taught constructive strategies to manage, the focus of intervention should be on the other children and adults

so that they can be more empathic and attuned to the socially unique requirements of the child with Autism.

- Self-esteem may arise from a sense of responsibility and reverence by others. The child with Autism who is focussed on moral values, rules and duty can be a natural leader. This can work well in the earlier years but as the child and peers grow older, it can lead to resentment, disregard and marginalisation. While it is important for the child with Autism to be given responsibility, these tasks need to be carefully chosen and modified according to the developmental age as well as feedback from the wider social group.

- The child with Autism should be informed of the diagnosis early on. This is unlikely to be psychologically harmful particularly if it is framed as an alternative way of thinking rather than a disorder. An earlier disclosure also facilitates trust between adult and child. However, there are certain labels that should be avoided such as Gifted and Professor. This not only creates a sense of confusion of identity for the child but places inappropriate expectations on performance as a measure of success.

- The importance of extra physical space, mental space and time for the sensory needs of the child with Autism must not be underestimated. The concept of time for the child with Autism may also be very different from others and this needs to be taken into consideration when developing a schedule of activities. Their notion of time may be non-linear based on priorities rather than o'clock time or there may be an extremely rigid concept of linear time with any deviations causing stress and anxiety.
- The notion that a child with Autism is content to be alone is not always accurate. It may be the case during sensory breaks for self-regulation. However, many more desire connection and relationship with others. They wish to fit in and be like everyone else. The boundaries of the family cannot be rigid. There needs to be regular exposure of the family to a broad range of nourishing neurotypical social activities in which the child with Autism can learn by mimicry and observation. Parents with Autistic tendencies who prefer social isolation, or interactions with a

circumscribed range of friends, need to be aware that this can negatively impact their child's development.

- Children with Autism can make extremely loyal and dedicated friends. However, they are prone to becoming obsessive and possessive. Eventually, this will destroy any friendships and lead to feelings of rejection or abandonment. The child then adopts the safer path of not having friendships to prevent any devastating feelings of loss. These tendencies need to be openly discussed with the child from the outset and excessive focus on just one best friend should be discouraged.
- Special interests play a crucial role as natural antidotes for stress and anxiety. The child with Autism needs regular opportunities to escape into a fantasy world such as Science Fiction. This can bolster self-esteem and creativity. Adults should not discourage their child from engaging in fantasy play based on shows that they may have seen. The possibility of Autism should not be discounted even though the child may appear to have an active imaginary world.

- Duty, compliance, respect towards elders and authority are prerequisites in a traditional Asian upbringing. For these children with Autism, the adults should be aware that they then can subtly push the child into areas of interest that they are not comfortable with or not suited to them in the longer term. The child then develops an interest for the sake of others rather than themselves.
- Depression and suicidal thinking are real possibilities even in very young children. Adults should be aware of this particularly if there is a family history. The symptoms can be very different from adults and include irritability, defiance, increased rigidity, perfectionism, sleep disturbance and pain. The focus needs to be on the *prevention* of mental health issues and illness rather than waiting for problems to arise.
- The difference between religion and spirituality needs to be acknowledged for the child with Autism. A sense of that which is greater than themselves is more important than a set of religious rituals and doctrines that can trigger or exacerbate an Obsessive-Compulsive Disorder. For any rituals or routines to be

adaptive, they need to be a source of comfort rather than distress. They should not increase anxieties around guilt, shame and wrongdoing.
- Do not underestimate the value of animals for the child with Autism. They can provide unconditional approval and acceptance, a sense of initiative and responsibility as well as companionship in times of sorrow and isolation.
- Diet is the most important medication of all. You are what you eat. Be aware of the impact of gluten, dairy and processed sugar on behaviour and mental health.

Chapter Two
Connectivity in Autism

This has been the most difficult chapter to compose and I specifically left it to the last. I think this was due to the shame that I felt at not having many friends and that it would be impossible for me to write much about social connections as I have never been in a "relationship". This chapter also brought back painful memories of the tumultuous childhood years and widening contrast that I felt to neurotypicals (people without Autism). Finding love can be hard for anyone, but perhaps more so for a person with Autism. I researched online and consulted with several neurotypical and neurodiverse (people with Autism) colleagues from the medical and psychological profession. They kindly provided guidance and inspiration on the issue of relationships in Autism. *Love on the Spectrum* also premiered on Internet TV at the time of writing of this chapter which was perfect to motivate me to tell my story about "the game of friendships and relationships" in Autism.

Indeed, I believe that developing and maintaining friendships or relationships is the most complex and perplexing issue affecting a person with Autism. Dealing with people does not come naturally as it comes with a burden of social and emotional confusion. I also grew up before the internet and online age. My upbringing was fairly religious with an Asian influence and complicated by social anxiety. This entailed a fear of being ridiculed, judged and of being the centre of attention. The Internet would have been a more comfortable space to share experiences, interests, thoughts and feelings without the confusing background of nonverbal social signals and sensory stimuli. It was very draining having to analyse and observe in person rather than online. I really had to perfect the art of observation and mimicry.

My early childhood memories of Malaysia included the image of my mother lying in bed pregnant with my sister, a caterpillar falling from the rambutan tree over my head, playing pranks on my maids and the succession of uncles who came to live with us to complete their pre-university studies. Another stand out memory was Kuching Kolo Mee, a local noodle dish of which I would have consumed two to three gluten loaded bowls a day as well as Ice Kachang, a red bean dessert. This was our family activity as we ventured to the hawker stalls at night or after church on Sundays. It was remarkable that I did not have issues with my weight from all the carbohydrates and sugar consumed.

Kuching Kolo Mee

Ice Kachang

I was obsessed with science fiction shows, namely Battlestar Galactica, Buck Rogers in the 25th Century, Star Trek, Star Fleet and Star Wars. My imagination and fantasy world revolved around spaceships, aliens and pretend friends. I was described as smart, kind, compassionate, clever, honest, quirky, quiet, shy, sensitive, an A student and a true gentleman. I was a listener rather than a talker. I desperately wanted friends but either did not know how to make and keep them or was too afraid of loss and thus chose the safety of solitude instead.

Recess and any unstructured times of the school day were particularly stressful socially when I was no longer Monitor or Prefect and could not be in control. There was bullying and rejection by the boys. I was recruited by several girls who were more supportive and friendships developed from having long phone conversations with them after school. In retrospect, speaking over the phone was safer and much more relaxing as I did not have to deal with the nonverbal cues necessary in face to face interactions.

I discovered that friendships have an expiry date. I was quite immature socially and had bursts of intense friendships characterised by absolute loyalty and dedication. I had strict definitions of what constituted a friend and was particularly sensitive to rejection. In the end, my best friends were my uncles, my grandmother, cat, books and BMX bicycle. My favourite books were Enid Blyton, Hardy Boys, Nancy Drew, Alfred Hitchcock and the Three Investigators. The BMX bicycle became my main mode of transportation and means of connectivity with the outside world. Journeys on my bicycle enabled me to observe people and how they interacted with each other.

With high school and adolescence, it became apparent that my intellectual growth far surpassed my social, emotional and sexual development. I gravitated towards likeminded peers who were either older or younger with similar interests but who were also socially awkward and less popular being in a single sex school. I was not invited to parties and academic achievements became my way of feeling good about myself. I was much more interested in the physical rather than social world. Books, studies and exams were my best friends. While other people dreaded exams, I thrived on them. I loved the adrenaline rush of preparing for tests, sitting for exams, getting the results and debating with the teachers any incorrect marking for bonus points. I was exposed to Medicine early through my own reading of medical encyclopaedias and attendance in hospital rounds, clinics and surgery with my Uncle. I had a Malay tutor, piano teacher and an English tutor who refined my English accent. While this should have led to much satisfaction and gratitude, I still felt a sense of emptiness, a void that could not seem to be filled no matter how much I excelled.

A person with Autism can find it difficult to know what love is. I simply did not know how to get started. I was not interested in sex and was terrified about even the thought of going on a date. All I wanted at the time was someone to look at cars with. I went to the car yards with the hope of meeting someone there to share my life with. My mother gave me two love ducks for my bed presumably with the hope that I would find someone. I have never considered myself by nature a romantic person. Dating, kissing, dancing, intimacy and sex sounded quite disgusting frankly. However, it was saddening for me to observe close relationships and intimacy form in others around me, including my sister and my lack of ability to be in a relationship with someone. As I was frequently bullied and called names such as nerd and gay, I was determined to put on a masculine façade. I purposefully changed my gait to walk more like a macho. I told others about my interest in girls when at the time, I was either not interested in anyone or curious about both genders. I created a fantasy world of girlfriends, boyfriends and families. I was so filled with shame that I made up being a father with a wife and children whom I could relate well with.

There was quite a bit of pressure to have a girlfriend from my immediate and external family. I was beginning to feel like a failure if I did not get married and be like everyone else. Yet, I struggled with the questions, "How do I have a girlfriend? Am I gay as people have teased me about?" I desperately wished to have my own family with children, a partner with whom I could share my innermost thoughts and feelings. In retrospect, this led to periods of depression in adolescence. I developed a stance of asexuality, not wanting to be in a relationship with either, feeling that it was better to be safe and alone than sorry from any feelings of loss or abandonment if relationships failed. In effect, my sexuality was repressed. I also found myself gravitating towards the company of adults and younger peers. I seemed to get along much better with them and over the years have come to realise that this is quite common in Autism although in certain contexts would be considered as unusual or weird.

There are numerous parallels between one's Autism identity and sexual identity. For those on the spectrum who struggle with their sexuality, there is a double whammy as I call it of being on the Autism spectrum and the LGBTQIAPK (Lesbian, Gay, Bisexual, Transgender, Queer or Questioning, Intersex, Asexual, Pansexual, Kink) spectrum. I believe that one's journeys in both spectrums go hand in hand. As long as one remains sexually confused, there will always be difficulties accepting yourself for who you are, whether you are Autistic or not, but much more so if you are.

In my last year of high school, love and relationships were placed on the back burner as I became super focussed on getting sufficient marks to enter Medicine in university. As much of a distraction as that was, the year was also the most challenging emotionally. I was away from my cat and found it deeply lonely and depressing being away from home. Waiting for public transport and sitting in the bus with the crowds to get to and from school was anxiety provoking. The school library was my safe haven for solitude. I made few friends that year although my cohort consisted of mature aged students from a variety of cultural backgrounds. I had the opportunity to keep up my Malay with the student groups from Malaysia and Indonesia. My English as a Second Language teacher seemed particularly fond of me and she made it a point to take me out after my exams with her husband for some sightseeing.

I spent most of the time in my bedroom listening to music and singing pieces from musicals such as Phantom of the Opera as a natural antidote for depression. I also took up mowing the lawn, solo walks to the park, washing cars, visiting the news agency to look at car magazines and the local video store. The visual splash of the video cassettes and discs was amazing and to this day I am deeply saddened by the demise of the video store. I really loved classic films, musicals, Science Fiction particularly Star Trek and even horror movies at one stage.

At this point, I should clarify that while the words loneliness and social isolation are often used interchangeably, there are important differences between the two. Social isolation refers to a lack of contact with other individuals, while loneliness is the feeling of being emotionally disconnected from others. Therefore, a person can be in the presence of others, even in a crowd and still feel lonely. I felt both socially isolated and lonely, even though it was the loneliness that troubled me the most.

I would like to acknowledge the support that my grandmother and auntie provided in my first year away from home. They prepared all my meals and made life as comfortable for me as possible. I am not sure how aware they were of my emotional struggles but I am deeply grateful to them for looking after me. Our weekend outings after church to the local Chinese restaurant for lunch specials and any social gatherings at home for my auntie's friends were my only means of social connectivity at the time. The year also gave me the opportunity to develop a separate identity from my parents which was an important milestone. Never forget the positives no matter how lonely the circumstances.

Tips:

- Whether you are a male or female person with Autism, you can still look for and fall in love. To love and be loved is at the core of being human and a powerful force in a person's life. I would rate it is at least 10/10 in importance. Contrary to popular belief, a person with Autism can be very affectionate and loving.
- There should be a balance of male and female friends which is best achieved through coeducational schooling. I felt more accepted in primary school which was coeducational than high school.
- Quality friendships and shared experiences of intimacy can serve as an important antidote for depression, loneliness and anxiety. Amongst the pseudo antidotes which worked for me at the time were studying and cleaning the car but they were never a satisfactory replacement for animal and/or human companionship. Look closely within your circle as to who could be your true friend and do not be afraid to reach out, online or offline. This can mean the difference between a life of solitude and fruitful companionship. You simply cannot sit idly and wait

for the person to magically appear in your life. Use special interests as a way of making friendships but be aware that there will be difficulties with keeping friendships when the interests of your friends change.

- While obesity is a major public health concern, new research suggests that there are two bigger threats: loneliness and social isolation. These can increase the risk of premature death by up to 50 percent! Unfortunately, technology and social media have become a replacement for face to face interactions. Electronic connectivity has paradoxically reduced real world connections which are critical for overcoming loneliness and emotional disconnection. I believe it is crucial for health and educational professionals to check a person's level of social connectedness and intervene early.

- Be polite, treat everyone with respect and have a non-judgemental attitude. Smile, make eye contact, use the person's name, give sincere compliments and encourage the other person to talk about their interests. We are more likely to win friends by showing interest in the passions and interests of others than by getting others interested in us. I realise that this is not within the comfort zone of a person with Autism but work on shifting attention away from self (which can exacerbate social anxiety) and instead focus on others.

- Consider carefully whether it would be better to date a neurotypical (person without Autism) or neurodiverse person and whether or when one should disclose Autism. I believe that you should be guided by your sixth sense. Whether or not you talk about Autism is less important than the connection and ability to relate to the other person on the same wavelength at your first and subsequent encounters. A match of your personality and interests is far more important than the level of Autism and the need to disclose.
- As far as dating scripts are concerned, be prepared for silences. Have no particular expectations. State at the beginning that the focus is on each other's company, rather than talking and if there is talking, focus on mutually agreed areas of special or joint interest. When in doubt, tell the truth and be honest about how difficult making conversation can be. Honesty is the best policy.

- Depending on your individual circumstances, a small dose of alcohol may help ease the tension during a date but should not be used as an antidote for ongoing social anxiety.
- Choose a setting that is informal, quiet and 1:1. Accept the possibility that any script that you have rehearsed can disappear from your mind due to anxiety. However, this should not prevent you from having fun recording yourself roleplaying conversation starters and keeping it going while still being yourself.
- I strongly recommend exploration of your sexuality and coming out (disclosure of sexual orientation or gender identity) if you are also on the LGBTQIAPK (Lesbian, Gay, Bisexual, Transgender, Queer or Questioning, Intersex, Asexual, Pansexual, Kink) spectrum. This can occur with a friend, Mentor, Coach or Psychologist. There are anonymous phone lines that provide sexuality counselling and support groups for persons with Autism who are gender diverse.

- Be prepared to honour Yes and No in any relationship. A person with Autism can be emotionally and sexually immature, which means that you can be vulnerable to being used, manipulated and abused. If you feel uncomfortable, particularly if the person seems to be after sex or your money, it is alright to end the relationship and move on.
- Connectivity in Autism includes relationships not just with people but with food, work, studies, your health, animals and money. How you do one thing is how you do everything.

Chapter Three
A university student with Autism

Allow me to share with you the issue of surviving and thriving with Autism as a university student. I will talk about the different subjects I learnt, expand on which ones were conducive to the Autism mind, which were not and why. On a practical note, I will provide suggestions on coping with assessments, examinations, applying for special consideration and working in an environment which involves significant interaction with others.

My experience of this crucial phase of my life could not be more aptly illustrated by what was written about me by a friend for graduation. In the list of the most memorable moments in Medical School, my name was mentioned several times; the gale force sneezes, when I asked permission from the lecturer to go to the toilet and the person with the cleanest car.

This anecdote reads as follows:

"I first made the acquaintance of Jonathan at a Physiology practical tutorial. I am pleased to announce that I still hold the esteemed status of being one of his acquaintances after an eventful five and a half years.

The key features in his biopsychosocial profile include:
- A style of elocution that would make a British monarch envious
- A fan of Star Trek, Star Wars, Babylon 5 and the Sound of Music
- Remarkable ability to memorise extensive passages in textbooks in one sitting
- Obsessive tidiness and daily cleaning of his car
- Natural talent for Psychiatry but they probably need a Medical Oncologist more in Kuching
- Strong belief in the maxim, "A medical student should be where he gains the most benefit."
- Very persistent in achieving his goal
- Obstinately difficult to repay for any acts of kindness
- Notably winning the Microbiology and Parasitology prizes.

Over the years, those in his clerkship group have been privileged to be entertained by his superb oratory style whenever he presents material in any academic setting. This, coupled with his excellent memorising ability, have left many medical consultants and examiners with their mouth agape in amazement after they have witnessed his performances.

However, under this outward persona of an ultra-self-disciplined and efficient medical student, there is still a part of Jonathan, which remains a bit of an enigma. There are parts of his personality and history which have eluded analysts and inquirers for years (although most of you are already diagnosing OCPD=Obsessive Compulsive Personality Disorder). So, who is this Jonathan character, really?

Using the evidence I have gathered over five and a half years of intense research and many hours of taped interviews, I have come to the conclusion that he is probably just a normal person from Kuching, East Malaysia, making his way through medical school. (Believe that and you'll believe anything.....freedom of speech is obviously not being allowed here.)

On a more serious note, despite the many secrets which I have been restrained from divulging to you, he has been a good friend, and I look forward to maybe one day visiting him wherever his practice may be".

Despite the emotional, social and sensory dilemmas, Medical School provided me with a sense of optimism about the future and proved to be one of the most satisfying periods of my life. Taking a step back, the entry process is very different to what it is like nowadays. At the time, the entrance criteria were solely based on high school exit examination scores. The higher the score, the greater the likelihood of securing a place in Medical School. In today's terms, I would have needed an aggregate score of at least 99% across all subjects to be offered a place.

I received the results of my university entrance examinations while I was on holiday in Malaysia. Based on my school examination results, I was simultaneously hoping and expecting to be offered a place. The question was which university as I had applied to several, in addition to Engineering being my second option. I could not recall feeling more elated at being offered a place in my first choice.

My memories of Orientation Day were positive despite the anxiety of meeting new people and my enduring awkwardness in group situations. I felt at home early on, being in a group of students who looked very intellectual, studious and dare I say, nerdy or geeky. I made my first friend outside the library, being impressed by his large bag and collection of badminton rackets.

As a reward for getting into university, my parents very generously purchased my first car. It was a Mazda 121, notably known as the Bubble Car for its bubbly shape. I was thrilled to be able to drive a car with power steering and a factory installed radio and cassette player. The air-conditioning system, so crucial to my heat sensitivities, was superb. It was however a manual, which I did not mind at the time. Manuals are better to improve focus while driving. It did not have central locking. There were no power windows either, all of which would be regarded as standard in today's cars. It was striking in a red colour called Passion Rose. I looked after it diligently, even obsessively. It was cleaned daily and was arguably truly the shiniest looking car in the parking lot anywhere on the university grounds.

Mazda 121

The race for a free parking spot in the mornings was a competitive event. I had to leave home at 0630 in the mornings to arrive before 0700. There were only a limited number of all-day free parking spots for several hundred students. On days when lectures start at 1000 or 1100, it meant a wait for several hours. If one missed out on free parking, it would mean the added stress of paying for parking or beating the dreaded parking inspector for every two or three hours of free roadside parking.

In those days, number plate recognition technology was of course not available. The parking inspector would use chalk to mark the tyres. Astute students would rush out of lectures or the library to shift the tyres to hide the chalk marks.

It was during this time that I developed a deeper attachment to my car. It became a place of solitude and withdrawal where I could shut myself away from any sensorially aversive environments (bright lights, noise of chatter, movement, smell of people). I listened to music, read my books and even slept (with a pillow) in the early winter morning races for a car spot. There were many times when I felt lonely too, as I observed the other students walking in groups, going out for lunch or being picked up by their family.

Despite the intellectual rewards and the preclinical years of Medical School being more sensorially friendly, it was still an emotionally challenging time. I still had no interest in romantic relationships. I had few friends which I at the time referred to as acquaintances. However, I am now truly grateful to these friends who have come to my aide several times in my life to provide much needed support in overcoming challenges.

In hindsight, it was joint special interests that enabled me to socially connect with others. I joined a Star Trek and Science Fiction Club which was run once a month on Fridays in another university. Each club meeting consisted of merchandise trading and screening of the two latest episodes of Star Trek The Next Generation, Star Trek Voyager or Babylon 5 from the USA. I also joined the university recreation centre for badminton and tennis. These were sports that I had undertaken as a child and found less confronting as they were not team based.

Food not only provided nourishment but became a means of engaging with others as well. I particularly looked forward to Kentucky Fried Chicken All You Can Eat Buffets on Fridays. For around $10, you could have as much KFC, coleslaw, chips and mashed potatoes as your heart desired. I believe I still hold the record of 18 pieces of KFC in the one sitting.

Kentucky Fried Chicken

The friendships that I developed could be described as quirky. One of my friends clearly had a case of Narcolepsy. This is a potentially dangerous condition where one falls asleep suddenly in any context. I almost always sat next to him at the very front of the lecture theatres. He often swayed from side to side before nodding off much to the amusement of the lecturers. He loved second hand bookshops and had a marvellous collection of phone cards which I later inherited. I enjoyed playing badminton outside the university libraries and re-enacting the script from the Sound of Music with him.

Another friend also had unusual hobbies, obsessions or in more diplomatic terms, passions. He was a Master at Chinese and Western Chess. He had biscuits for breakfast daily and was still able to maintain a lean figure. His home (and his birds) which was near university became a regular place for lunch catch ups, table tennis and examination preparation.

On an intellectual note, I had come from a situation of being the top student in my high school to a humbler student with many others who were smarter and who had achieved higher scores in the entrance examinations. I was in a highly competitive environment and this was not limited to competition for a car parking spot in the mornings. However, it was this competition and periods of loneliness that motivated me to put my best into my studies. According to the Faculty Dean at the time, Medicine is a process of lifelong learning. Studying, which I had discovered as a child, became a definite special interest. This learning became the most potent antidote for depression and anxiety. Excellence in studies as well as examinations defined me and gave me a strong sense of self-worth. Studying became an enjoyable hobby which was extremely valuable, helping me to relax.

I will now consider each subject in turn, their conduciveness to the Autism mind and the ones that I particularly excelled in. These appeared to be subjects that made the best of my Obsessive-Compulsive traits. They were also subjects where fitting in was not the centre of the learning experience. Please note that the curriculum has evolved over the years and it has not been possible for me to cover every subject a medical student would encounter nowadays.

Medical Chemistry

Chemistry was a forte from high school so this subject with its focus on the natural sciences came easily to me. Rote learning of various chemical equations was essential, and I easily obtained a Distinction grade.

Behavioural Sciences, Public Health and General Practice

This subject in the preclinical years was a sound introduction to my skills as a budding Social Scientist. I felt an immediate connection to the subject and the lecturer. I sadly missed out on the sex education videos and was thrilled to have had the opportunity to undertake sit ins and home visits with a General Practitioner.

I was introduced to the concept of systems theory (which referred to how individuals in a system depended on each other to achieve particular goals). This was easier to learn than the critical reviews and analysis assignments which were part of the Public Health Component. It is likely that my Autism mind struggled with that part as it depended on higher order critical thinking skills and mathematical calculations which were in stark contrast to the rest of the unit material. In other words, it was difficult for me to shift instantaneously from being a black and white thinker to a "shades of grey thinker" which was a requirement of this unit. Despite this, the extra effort and time I invested to train my brain to think flexibly scored me a Distinction grade as well.

Medical Biomorphology

Biology was also a strength from high school, so this unit was a relatively easy undertaking. It required a great deal of rote learning. Unfortunately, there was a chickenpox outbreak in Medical School which led to a rather miserable time dealing with chicken pox lesions. I also did not enjoy the foetal pig dissection labs due to the sensorially aversive smell of the preserved pig. Therefore, this unit was challenging because of illness and difficulties coping with sensory issues.

Physiology and Biophysics

Physics was unfortunately a relative weakness, despite many others on the Autism Spectrum having a natural inclination for the subject. Humour was a very important coping skill. The Biophysics lecturer was a classic absent-minded Professor. There was one occasion when the lecture theatre phone rang incessantly but he was unable to locate the phone moving from one to the next.

Darth Vader's (fictional character from Star Wars®) Physiology was a crucial metaphor to survive this subject which again required a huge effort in rote learning. Fortunately, my visual memory was a strength and I was able to mentalise the function of various bodily systems such as the flow of the urinary system and conduction of the nervous system. I had a remarkable visual memory consistent with the finding that individuals with Autism are usually visual rather than auditory learners.

With regards to Darth Vader, it became a joint interest for me and several colleagues. Many library sessions were spent postulating on how his lungs worked and the mechanics of his ventilatory device. It is said that Laughter is the Best

Medicine and the impersonations that we made of Darth Vader helped me survive this unit well. Mimicry, copying and immersing oneself in the persona of others is a strength for a person with Autism.

Human Anatomy

Unfortunately, this subject was a challenge like the foetal pig dissection labs. This was due to the sensory problems associated with the overpowering smell of formalin used to preserve the cadaver (corpse). There were several students who fainted, and I was the only student who wore a surgical mask to reduce the intensity of the smell. I also experienced a burning sensation to the eyes. I did not enjoy the labs at all but was determined to make the best of my Obsessive-Compulsive traits. My duty was to read out the dissection manual for the group with the highest level of elocution and to impress the Radiology Tutor with my knowledge of Anatomy as we went through relevant X Rays.

Coordinated Neurosciences

I obtained a Distinction grade for this subject which introduced me to the workings of the human brain. This was a subject that resonated very well with my Autism mind. Despite the ongoing sensory challenges of examining the human brain that had been dosed with formalin, I made copies of the videos that came with the lectures and found them extremely helpful in visualising and internalising (remembering) the details. The smell of the brain thus proved to be a powerful trigger to my memory for how parts of the brain looked and how they worked.

Clinical Microbiology and Laboratory Medicine

This subject was highly conducive to the Autism mind. It dealt with germs (bacteria, viruses, fungi, parasites) and fuelled my obsessive-compulsive traits in a positive way. I was utterly fascinated with the germs and spent many hours researching the topic. I was able to visualise each of their appearances through my eidetic (photographic) memory. In order to remember the colourful yet complex names, I recorded all my notes on a portable cassette recorder, listened to them during sleep and while driving to and from university. This technique appeared to engrain an enormous amount of factual information into the unconscious and enabled me to obtain a Distinction grade.

A portable recorder to remember the microbes

Medical Pharmacology

The highlight of this subject was not the subject matter but the way in which it was presented by an extremely quirky and funny Professor of Medicine. His use of the pointer as a laser gun to wake up sleepy medical students was fondly remembered. Once again, humour proved to be an important coping mechanism for a relatively dry subject.

Pathology

This subject required a tremendous amount of discipline and rote learning. In the preclinical years, it was probably the subject that needed the biggest "elephant's memory". It was also conducive to the Autism mind, not only because of my detailed visual memory but the highly structured nature of its content. Each disease had its subject matter divided into distinct headings. There was a clear relationship between theory (for example, appearance and cause) and how this information could be useful in clinical practice (for example, signs and symptoms as well as prognosis).

Importantly, it was not socially demanding as the study involved many hours peering into the microscope and laboratory work in the basement which did not have any windows.

The biggest challenge was becoming consumed in the detail, the eidetic memory which produced confronting images of disease as well as images of mutilated dead bodies from forensic pathology. Attendance in the Necropsy Labs which commenced at 0700 for one week was compulsory. I needed extra time to recharge and recover from the trauma of the visual onslaught.

General Practice

This was a refreshing subject that covered theory and demonstrated relevance in practice. It introduced me to the human condition and honed my skills as a Social Scientist. I was particularly interested in the opportunity to ask patient's questions about their experience of illnesses and the importance of family support in their recovery. I took detailed notes from the General Practice clinics that I attended. I obtained a Distinction grade.

Psychiatry

I can only say that this subject came most naturally to me. I slipped into it with ease and was fascinated by the patients that I came across. I felt like I was a born Social Scientist. It introduced me to the notion of working in teams which would apply to many other areas of Medicine and Surgery. It enabled me to formally practice the art of observation, which I learnt later is an important skill for any person on the spectrum. I spent time diagnosing my colleagues and teachers in addition to patients. I was able to zoom into the detail of the individual person and zoom out into the wider system in which the individual belonged.

While talking to people and listening to their problems would have been exhausting for many on the spectrum, I did not feel it at the time. I actually gained energy from "socialising" with others within a structured context in which I felt in control. Unfortunately, Autism was not on the radar at the time nor was it on the curriculum as far as I could remember. Instead, Obsessive Compulsive Disorder and Obsessive-Compulsive Personality Disorder seemed to be the most common findings from my retrospective analysis.

The teachings in Psychiatry also prepared me to deal with all different kinds of people. This included individuals who might be considered as antisocial or borderline. Little was I aware that as I became more attuned to the needs of others, I would eventually neglect my own. Overall, this was one of my favourite subjects for which I obtained a High Distinction grade.

Clinical Ethics

This was also an Autism friendly subject which appealed to the high moral virtues and black and white style of thinking of an individual on the spectrum. I enjoyed reading up, committing to memory various ethical scenarios and regurgitating the responses in assignments and examinations for which I obtained a Distinction. The nature of the mind with Autism is to think in black and white terms but a subject like Ethics can help it to expand and consider the shades of grey, as was the case for the subject matter on the limitations of making Psychiatric as opposed to other more objective forms of medical diagnoses.

Medicine

This subject was challenging by virtue of a teacher that I had to deal with. There were many who were supportive and nurturing, but I was unfortunate to have been placed in a group with a young doctor who took it upon his stead to bully the medical students. We had to stay past midnight for tutorials, and I felt so traumatised by the style of teaching that I avoided several sessions. I felt extremely guilty about missing any teaching but later learnt that it is often what you feel bad about doing that needs to be done for your own sake.

Bedside tutorials and ward rounds meant exposure to large groups which was confronting and mentally exhausting. I did not enjoy crowds which at the time I did not recognise as an Autistic trait. It was only the free lunches and merchandise that appealed to the students at the time. This encouraged attendance at weekly Grand Rounds where a lunch would be followed by a clinical presentation.

Despite the social and sensory challenges, my 1:1 bedside manner was impeccable, and I enjoyed individually clerking the patients for their history. I was often able to impress the tutors with my encyclopaedic knowledge and polished case presentations.

Medicine was my introduction to the practical demands of being a doctor. This included early starts, late finishes, long periods of standing during ward rounds, dealing with crowds and difficult people.

Paediatrics

It is said that if you are a person with Autism, you tend to relate better with individuals not your age. This includes people who are many years older than you or children. For this reason, Paediatrics appealed very much to my inner child which in retrospect was my Autistic self, striving to be discovered and nurtured.

The teachers were also very childish themselves with one I recall hanging upside down from the door to illustrate a point. Children are also non-judgmental and matter of fact. I found it very rewarding taking histories from them. The children's hospital had a fantastic library with learning stations that were very friendly from a sensory perspective. I was able to withdraw every lunch hour to recharge and engrossed myself in numerous journals and atlases. This was extremely important as the hospital environment is not at all sensorily friendly, with screaming babies, crying children and distraught parents which I can only describe as, "really cutting into you".

I subsequently learnt from my tutors that the greatest challenge in Paediatrics is having to deal with the parents and it was this that unconsciously turned me away from the Specialty at the time even though I obtained a Distinction grade.

Obstetrics and Gynaecology

I am still puzzled as to how I managed to score a Distinction for this subject. I would not have considered it Autism friendly as my term occurred over a sizzling summer and overnight sleeps in the nursing quarters while on call for deliveries. Babies could arrive at any time and labours could last a very very long time. Moreover, the smells associated with maternal and foetal body liquids were sensorially aversive. It is likely that the appeal to my inner child motivated me to persevere and succeed here.

Infectious Diseases

As with Clinical Microbiology and Laboratory Medicine, the study of germs came naturally and appealed to my obsessive-compulsive mind. I won the Prize for this subject and was honoured to have won an additional subspecialty

Parasitology prize from a founding Parasitologist. I received a book and medallion personally from him at his Nursing Home. This gesture instilled in me the importance of looking after our elderly and returning service to society by investing in the younger generation.

Clinical Pharmacology

Building on Medical Pharmacology from the preclinical years, Clinical Pharmacology which involved the study of drugs and its applications in clinical practice was an Autism friendly subject for which I scored a high distinction. It did not involve any significant person to person contact. Drug encyclopaedias became my closest friends at the time.

General Surgery

This subject in its broadest sense did not appeal to my Autism mind. In retrospect, it was not the subject matter but the sensory and emotional demands. I found it extremely tiring standing for prolonged periods in the surgical theatre with a group of people, coping with the smell of the diathermy blade (burning flesh and fat) and dealing with a few teachers who were not exactly friendly people. It may be a subject that appeals to some other individuals on the Autism Spectrum in that it involves fewer social interactions and the need to talk to patients. The outcomes are also black and white in nature with problems often solved by "cutting it out".

Anaesthesia

Despite the challenges I had with General Surgery, I enjoyed Anaesthetics very much. Drugs were an area of special interest and I was able to sit down in theatre. It is said that Anaesthesia is terror for 1% during the induction and boredom for 99% of the rest of the time. It was a good opportunity for me to catch up on reading while keeping an eye on the instruments and generally reflect on the things that I had learnt. There was also very little talking to asleep patients of course. I scored a Distinction grade and participated in a Prize Viva for this subject.

Otorhinolaryngology

A High Distinction grade in this subject suggests that Surgery, particularly as a subspecialty can be successful for a doctor with Autism. It was Autism friendly in that it involves zooming in on a very specific part of the body (ears, nose and throat), relatively little pressure to talk with patients for extended periods and the opportunity to sit down while operating.

Ophthalmology

It has been said that individuals on the Autism Spectrum do not experience physical blindness but a form of mind blindness. In this context, they are not able to see and respond appropriately to social cues. In other words, there is a reduced or even lack of ability in "putting others into our own shoes".

I would argue that there are others like me who see too much of the social cues and have a natural talent in immersing oneself in the mind of others. I found myself constantly analysing what my peers did, how they spoke, their body language, what I should think, feel and how I should react in every possible situation. In this sense, Ophthalmology also appealed to me at the time as it involves zooming in and extremely detailed analysis of a very specific part of the body. I obtained a Distinction grade for this subject.

Subject choice:

The conduciveness of a subject to the mind with Autism will also depend on one's learning, personality profile and associated anxiety (obsessive compulsive traits). Generally speaking, a subspecialty rather than generalist (for example General Medicine and General Surgery) subject will be easier to master. This is consistent with the Autism one-track mind and ability to zoom into the microscopic details. As I illustrated, it was not only the subject matter but perhaps more importantly the teacher and how the material was presented. In addition, my fear of germs swayed me towards subjects that did not require physical contact with patients. Psychiatry was the prime example.

Examinations:

On the subject of preparing for and dealing with examinations, the general principles that would apply to anyone such as early preparation, the use of study aides, visual and auditory learning methods, repeated exposure to the learning material and anxiety management would also apply to the mind with Autism. In clinical presentations, a key strategy has to do with the art of eye contact with the examiners. I suggest you look near their eyes and neck while the rest of the body still appears confident and calm. An avoidance of eye contact is a sign of poor examination technique and can lead to failure.

Disclosure and special consideration:

There were no special considerations for Autism during my time in Medical School. However, during my more recent postgraduate studies, I found it useful to disclose that I have Autism and Anxiety. This enabled me to obtain extra time for assignments and examinations, which was extremely helpful. I would strongly encourage you to disclose your diagnosis as soon as possible to individuals that you trust and relevant staff within the Faculty.

I believe that these special allowances are particularly necessary now given the additional challenges placed on the Autism mind with the evolution of the medical curriculum from didactic or rote based learning to one of integrated problem-based learning. Unfortunately, possessing encyclopaedic levels of knowledge is no longer enough to pass medical school. There is a lot more emphasis on the clinical application of this knowledge and presenting your findings to a group. The social and sensory demands are now even greater. The entrance process involves a face to face interview which was not a requirement during my time. I strongly suggest that adaptation is required for this process, similar to interviews for a workplace which are deemed unsuitable for individuals with Autism as it does not showcase their strengths. It is more beneficial for the individual to demonstrate their strengths via a short-term placement or via alternative media such as a series of videos.

In summary, my journey through Medical School was actually my personal therapeutic journey for Autism. I did not have to pay for anyone to provide me with support or treatment. It was a voyage that I had to carve out for myself.

I had to make the best of the resources that I had at the time and turned challenges in learning into opportunities.

Other student Tips:

- Arrange a baseline cognitive (IQ) and neuropsychological assessment (including executive functioning) before entering Medical School. This assessment can be completed by an educational psychologist. It is a worthwhile investment to identify strengths and relative weaknesses, identify any subtle language and comprehension difficulties, determine your learning profile and adaptations required.
- Join a university support group for students on the Autism Spectrum. This can even be an online group via e-mail, discussion forums and video group conversations.
- Research and participate in clubs in order to interact with others based on shared special interests.
- Connect with sensory anchors to motivate you to achieve your goals. Anchors can be something that you can see, a favourite smell or song. Other examples include post it notes to yourself or pictures of your strengths such as dedication, enthusiasm, persistence and discipline as well as areas of special expertise.

- Out of sight often becomes out of mind. Everything that you need to think of, use or do should be visually present.
- Listen to and respect the opinions of others, regardless of whether you agree with them or not. It is important to cultivate early the art of diplomacy and negotiation.
- Appearance and perception are all important. Always present with an attitude of optimism and enthusiasm, regardless of the circumstances.
- Avoid being judgemental of others. For example, focussing on the negative and criticising others. This can come across as narcissistic (self-centred, arrogant and inconsiderate).
- Do not assume what is on the person's mind. Do not be afraid to ask and clarify for yourself.
- Always take into consideration the context to identify the meaning behind the actions of others. It is usually not as bad as you think.
- Do not waste energy on things that are beyond your control. Continually ask yourself, "what can I do now, what can I learn from this and how can I turn this into a positive opportunity.

- Make sure you provide yourself with regular brain breaks to assimilate and absorb information. Use an application such as Big Stretch Reminder®. Program it to pop up every 30 minutes to remind yourself to have a movement break.
- Avoid getting consumed by the details particularly in technical areas, the tendency to micro analyse the meaning of every word and succumbing to obsessive slowness. Use a timer on your computer screen to set limits and prevent excessive or prolonged focus on a task.
- Rote learn chapter highlights, figures and summaries rather than everything.
- Make the best of alternative learning methods such as attending lectures online, presenting a case via video link and conducting interviews over the phone.
- Anxiety is part and parcel of life. Never let it get the better of you but rather use it to help you focus and overcome any problems.
- Be aware of your signs of stress: headaches, heaviness in the chest, a feeling of sensory overload, heartburn, hypervigilance of the environment, tunnel vision with

loss of awareness of the bigger picture, seeing too much of the bigger picture, increased obsessiveness, rigidity and perfectionism. Other common reactions to stress are anger or withdrawal, the latter in which you detach yourself and become emotionally numb. Have a Stress Action Plan in place with a step by step guide on what to do such as washing your face with cold water, breathing deeply, cleaning and having a break from electronics.

Chapter Four
Medicine's place in the Autism universe

Diversity is the notion that incorporates differences such as race, gender, ethnicity and sexuality. How a person perceives themselves and how they perceive others largely influences how they interact with other people. Neurodiversity refers to the idea that people may look the same but not think the same as opposed to diversity where people think the same even though they may not look the same. Persons diagnosed with Autism, Attention Deficit Hyperactivity Disorder (ADHD), Dyslexia and Tourette's Syndrome amongst others may choose to identify themselves as being on the neurodiversity spectrum by being neurodiverse or neurodivergent.

I believe that awareness and knowledge of neurodiversity in the medical profession is still in its infancy. Doctors do not seem to be as aware as they should be about their level of neurodiversity let alone that of their colleagues. Without this awareness and knowledge, would they be able to recognise it in their patients and support them to the best of their ability? Despite my quirks, not once did any of my colleagues or supervisors suggest that it would be worthwhile seeking an Autism assessment to assist with my professional awareness and development. In retrospect, this would have made an enormous difference to how I perceived myself, worked with others and importantly how I worked with my patients.

I would argue that this means that the recognition of Autism and anything else on the neurodiversity spectrum in doctors is fundamental to their personal and professional wellbeing, particularly in the area of mental health. The earlier this occurs, the better. However, doctors and those in the helping professions are likely to slip under the neurodiversity radar by "faking it", putting on a mask and presenting a façade of being a neurotypical (person not on the neurodiversity spectrum) by copying or mimicry. "Faking it" has been recognised as a significant stressor for a person with Autism. Immersing oneself into a role and not being who you really are is very draining. However, it became such an effective strategy for success as a junior doctor that I lost insight into why I was doing it, how it chipped away at my core sense of self and who I really was as a person.

I graduated from Medical School with Honours. This meant that I was among the top 10% of graduates. The first year of work, otherwise known as the internship was full of excitement and expectation. I was feeling good, perhaps even high with being a doctor. I had finally completed my studies and was getting paid. I had my first personal credit card and with the extra income, I could attend to my special interests and buy not just one but two cars in my first year. As for work, there are compulsory rotations that an Intern needs to complete. I had two terms of Emergency Medicine which lasted six months, three months of General Medicine and three months of General Surgery. My Registrars and Consultants (senior doctors) were full of praise for my dedication, reliability, dependability, attention to detail and amazing organizational skills. These can be Autism strengths and it was great that these were recognised early in my career despite the absence of a formal diagnosis. I was also fortunate at the time that no job interviews were required and I had chosen the most Autism friendly hospital environment to work in. This included an open ambience critical for sensory processing, easy parking, less crowds and closeness to the beach for walks.

A final year medical student was guaranteed a job provided they passed the year. Since then, interviews have become an essential part of the job application process, particularly to assess the would-be doctor's social and communication skills. Important questions that may be asked during the interview are what one's signs of stress are, coping mechanisms and emotional resilience. Unfortunately, these are areas that are not Autism strengths. Therefore, it is quite possible that a potentially talented doctor with Autism can fail the interview process without an awareness, particularly from the interviewers of the social and communication weaknesses that come with a neurodiverse mind.

As an Intern, one is at the bottom of the hospital hierarchy. It was not uncommon to be treated more as an object rather than a person. A junior doctor with Autism is vulnerable to bullying in the workplace, particularly if there is a lack of awareness of one's boundaries, a fear of failure and not being able to say no. This bullying can be quite subtle and much more likely to be emotional. Experiences of bullying in childhood can resurface at work, leading to increased trauma-based anxiety symptoms. Anxiety and depression often go hand in hand. When one occurs, the other is often not far away. A particular area of vulnerability was shift work and the ability to say no to working extra shifts. I found myself working extra for the sake of more money to pay the bills.

The year following the Internship is known as the Residency. For six months of that year, I worked as a Resident Medical Officer (RMO) in Medical Specialities such as Renal Medicine, Psychiatry and Emergency. Interestingly, the consistent shift work provided by Emergency and the ability to work with cases without developing an attachment to them given the high throughput meant that it was easier for me to cope as an undiagnosed doctor with Autism. For the remaining six months, I was promoted to work as a Medical Registrar, a position which was a struggle due to the high number of elderly people with falls, dizziness, strokes and "dyscopia" (inability to cope) that had to be seen every shift. There were nights when ten to twenty patients had to be reviewed for admission and bed availability was an ongoing problem.

During this time, I became conflicted between choosing a career in Medicine and applying for registrar training in Psychiatry. In the end, the financial incentive and more predictable working hours won the day. As an attraction and retention measure, registrars in Psychiatry were automatically promoted two pay grades and I could only think at the time about more money to spend on my special interests. I recall at the time that many people balked at the idea of my interest in Psychiatry due to the stigma associated with the profession. The usual response was, "why would you want to do that? Use your talents in another area of medicine!". I was also anxious about disclosing this to my parents as Psychiatry was not regarded as an esteemed speciality. There was a sense of shame that I had let them down. Yet, something persuaded me to continue.

Prospective applicants for Psychiatric training were screened with an hour-long interview. I came well prepared and had rehearsed for many days' potential questions and responses. The focus of the questions for me was "why Psychiatry?", experiences so far working with chronic health conditions and challenges working within a multidisciplinary team. My responses included a wish to help others, to combat the stigma associated with mental health, the importance of early intervention, recognising and dealing with conflict. All these responses were well rehearsed. A doctor with Autism who has performance skills as a forte can actually ace the interview process. If I had the opportunity to go through the process again, I would have reduced the façade, disclosed my level of neurodiversity, the significance of Psychiatry for my own personal mental health journey, the training college's experience in supporting trainees with neurodiverse issues, allowances and Autism specific support.

In my first year of Psychiatry training, I developed skills in Emergency Psychiatry in a busy metropolitan hospital Emergency Department, particularly patients with severe personality disorder and dual diagnosis (co-occurrence of mental disorders and substance abuse). I was trained in the flexible and clinically appropriate use of specific psychiatric assessment guides. I attained and consolidated the ability to structure, probe and cross examine. This structured approach to psychiatric interviews and being a social detective resonated very well with the Autism mind.

My supervisor for that year, an eminent Professor of Psychiatry recognised me as one of the best trainees ever to have worked with him. My performance was rated in writing as in the top quintile of first year trainees, in the top 10% of trainees with regards to diagnostic interviewing skills and ability to summarise clinical information in writing. Documentation and discharge summaries, crucial in the job description of a junior trainee were rated as exemplary.

In my second year of training, I had the opportunity to work in child, adolescent and old age mental health. There are numerous parallels between the two opposite ends of the developmental spectrum, particularly the importance of working with the family. My special interest in working with younger and older persons became particularly strong that year. My supervisors at the time strongly encouraged me to undertake subspecialty training in either Child and Adolescent Psychiatry or Psychogeriatrics. The latter deterred me due to the incurable notion of dementia, dealing with dying and the inability to communicate with most of the patients seen.

That year, I developed and ran a group programme for adolescent inpatients and day patients in conjunction with a Clinical Psychologist and Clinical Pharmacist. This programme focused on adolescent identity formation, the role of medications in their overall management and working with their motivation to maintain adherence, often easier said than done when working with teenagers. I also saw older teenagers and young adults with first episode psychosis (first time in a person's life of loss of touch with reality, fixed beliefs, disjointed thoughts and hallucinations), dual diagnosis and emotionally unstable personality disorders. Patients included Aboriginal people, migrants and refugees from the Eastern Mediterranean Region. I presented cases to General Practitioners to facilitate ongoing partnerships between primary, secondary (outpatient clinic based) and tertiary (hospital inpatient based) care.

In short, I was convinced that the mental health of young people was my calling, as many of their challenges resonated with what I had gone through as a child and that helping them would give me the opportunity to change their life course so that they would not have to go through what I did. Providing them with a voice and choice, communicating and networking with various elements of the health system to advocate for their needs including setting up interview rooms more conducive to psychiatric interviewing of children, learning skills in systemic therapy, psychotherapy and family therapy, teaching junior doctors was my own self-initiated and maintained therapy.

My years as a trainee in Child and Adolescent Psychiatry were mostly fulfilling. The work that was done was a great boost to my self-esteem and in retrospect, helped put my life in perspective. No matter how difficult your life circumstances are, there will always be others in more challenging situations. There is the opportunity for early intervention and less of a sense of hopelessness that can come with the chronic cases seen in adult mental health. Moreover, whilst you need to be responsible for what you do, your Consultant is the person who holds ultimate clinical responsibility.

As a senior trainee, you will inevitably be called upon to supervise more junior doctors and teach medical students. While it was good to have a sense of being able to teach others and share your knowledge, I found it difficult to cope with doctors and students whom I felt did not perform to "standard". This was likely to be due to a mismatch between not just the personality of the trainee and myself but the Autism aspect of communication and behaviour. This situation is likely to be exacerbated if you do not share the teaching responsibilities with another doctor who is not on the spectrum.

The most challenging aspect of working as a trainee with Autism was being on call, after hours work and dealing with office politics. I will speak about these in turn. As a Registrar on call, you will often be called in by the Emergency Department to deal with parents who are unable to cope with angry or aggressive boys and teenage girls who have self-harmed by cutting or overdose. These calls can occur at any time, particularly on weekends and when there was a full moon (despite the controversial evidence, I personally saw a relationship between the full moon and disturbed behaviour). Generally speaking, school holidays tended to be quieter periods with the absence of school demands as stressors or precipitants to emotional and behavioural meltdowns. During a bad night, particularly in adult mental health, you could have up to 10 patients waiting to be seen, usually for a risk assessment. This takes its toll on anyone but particularly so if you are a doctor with Autism. Fortunately, additional safeguards are in place for junior doctors nowadays.

I personally experienced office politics (the "mind and emotional games" at work) as perplexing and confusing. Envy can arise from your colleagues if your work performance is held in high regard and becomes the benchmark. I was a young doctor who completed my training in record time and often ended up supervising other doctors who were much older than me. In the area of public mental health, there can be competition between different disciplines, particularly in the area of child and adolescent mental health. The boundaries between what a Psychiatrist does and what a Social Worker, Psychologist and Occupational Therapist can do are often blurred. The Psychiatrist may end up in the narrow role of medication reviews and prescriptions. As the trainee, you are then likely to end up being in a position of doing this task as your main duty, i.e. the go to person for scripts. I would argue that the role of a Child and Adolescent Psychiatrist is much broader than this and while office politics and professional envy needs to be accepted as a part of working life, a doctor with Autism who has come out as being on the spectrum should be blunt in pointing out the elephant in the room and speaking the unspeakable as far as team dynamics and professional rivalry is concerned. Being blunt is an Autism trait that your work colleagues may actually find refreshing and thus your team should be educated and encouraged to be supportive of this trait.

I was fortunate enough to have a supervisor who was very much into toilet humour and the sort of stuff that young children would have giggles about. This included poking fun at names, bottoms on fire, toilets getting blocked, farts and phallic symbols. While there is a danger in taking things too far and offending others, especially females on the team, a healthy dose of humour was critical to bring lightness to the team, muscle relaxation and detoxification from the environmental stressors at work.

When all else fails, pets can be a powerful antidote for calming any unpleasant dynamics and office politics. Animals can also be very therapeutic for a person with Autism. During my training years, I was a strong advocate for a fish tank in the waiting room and a cat for the outpatient clinic (provided staff did not have insurmountable allergies of course). Animals are not judgemental and often the best judge of character.

Tips:

- The key to finding the best employer who recognises you for who you are, your skills and your talents is to make sure that you are as well aware of them as you can yourself. You are your own best guide.
- Consider workplace disclosure of a pending or actual diagnosis of Autism early. This will help you to gauge how suitable the work environment will be for you and what supports are likely to be provided.
- Your Curriculum Vitae (CV) may include a section on neurodiversity, its benefits to the workplace in terms of academic skills, responsibilities, achievements, leadership and management strengths.
- Guidelines should be developed for screening and supporting undiagnosed and diagnosed medical students and doctors with Autism. Employers need to build up their awareness of Autism and appreciate that what often appears as an attitude problem usually turns out to be a communication problem. While rules, policies and procedures can provide the Autism mind with much needed structure and security, it can be

misperceived as being excessively rigid and formal in the minds of some people without Autism.

- Workplace employment processes and specialty training interviews should include a mandatory question about experience with diversity, including neurodiversity. Disclosure, if appropriate can then follow.
- Interviews should not be used as the key employment strategy for doctors with Autism. An opportunity to demonstrate skills through two to four weeks of a work trial period would be in line with initiatives to employ people with Autism in other professions.
- Regardless of your level of Autism, the key to employment happiness and success is a good match between your skills, your job and a good enough match between you and the people in the workplace.
- Life as a junior doctor will involve a combination of work, study and preparation for specialist exams. The principles of preparing for exams in medical school still apply. Importantly, role play, practise cases every day, master the theory and use Mentors who can support you as exam coaches. Watch other candidates

in action (in person and online) and use this period as an opportunity to perfect your Autism skills of observation and mimicry. Familiarise yourself with the exam environment before the actual exams by visiting the site and make an attempt to sit in the actual exam area as an exposure exercise for anxiety. Do not take failure personally and criticise yourself for it. Consider failures as opportunities for growth and transformation.

- A junior doctor with Autism would have performed better in older examination formats where the focus was more on rote learning and unobserved interviews. The shift to problem-based learning, OSCEs (Objectively Structured Clinical Examinations) and OCIs (Observed Clinical Interviews) is more difficult for the Autism mind. A lot more practice and specific intervention to address anxiety should be considered, including Cognitive Behaviour Therapy, Hypnosis and medication.

- Medicine can be an important focus of your life but do not make it your life in totality. An obsession with work and having work as your sole relationship is not a wise idea. The more you fake it, the weaker your sense of self becomes.

- Beware of danger when you feel like you are working 24/7 or 365 days of the year or are telling others that you are doing so. Accept your limitations. You are not invincible. Although hyper focus and persistence is very useful at work, it can cause problems with your health. Imagine a stop button. Without one, you can go far beyond your capabilities and make yourself sick in the process.
- Beware of the Universal Halo Effect. People may assume that just because you excel in one thing, you are excellent in all other areas. This is a potentially detrimental assumption to your own wellbeing.
- Block off time to meet up with family and persons not in the medical profession.
- Do not underestimate the significance of positive lifestyle measures on your health as a junior doctor. *You are how you sleep and eat.* Consistent sleep is paramount for the Autism mind. I strongly advocate for doctors with Autism to have flexible working hours and starts depending on their innate circadian

rhythm (body clock). For a person who is an early riser, an early start and finish is recommended (e.g., 0700-1600). For a person who rises late and goes to bed late, a late start and finish would be more appropriate (e.g., 1100 to 2000).

- Other workplace accommodations that you should consider seeking from your employer include coping with hyper or hyposensitivity (to sound, lighting etc) which requires careful planning as prevention is better than cure. Ask for the flexibility to attend meetings via phone or video link as much as possible to reduce the stress associated with face to face interactions. Ask for a Mentor who can meet with you in private at least weekly to help you interpret the office politics, staff dynamics and warn you if the Autism is taking control of you instead of you being in control of the Autism. Ask for a pet at work and special consideration for on call and overnight work commitments. Ask for a job share arrangement with another doctor who is a good match to your personality and Autism talents. This doctor does not necessarily need to be neurotypical or neurodiverse (with Autism).

What is more important is the match between you two. A job share arrangement means that you can both be on the lookout for each other and cover for each other when needed.

- Team meetings are energy draining as it is hard to follow multiple lines of thought and analyse the body language of many people at once. Focus on staying relatively quiet, jot down notes to formulate and synthesise the information in writing before presenting it in the middle and towards the end. Speaking less can give the perception of being intelligent. Detox after each team meeting by going to your private personal space to undertake a relaxing activity or a walk. Think about flipping a coin when you need to change your mindset. Joining the meeting by phone or video link is a reasonable alternative.
- Have an attitude of collaboration and cooperation when working in teams. Avoid the us vs me mentality.
- The best antidote that I discovered for promoting team cohesion was humour. Use your quirky Autism sense of humour to bring lightness to the team.

- Opportunities for healthy sexual release is a crucial and not talked about lifestyle measure. Any young person, including a young doctor with Autism is a sexual being too. Beware of addictions to sex and pornography during this time. Movement, exercise and a pet are potent antidotes.
- A person with Autism goes to work to work rather than socialise. Recognise that water cooler and lunch conversations are crucial social activities and make an attempt to engage in these once a week. The people at work are likely to become your second family so invest in developing positive relationships with them.
- Do not feel pressured to engage in gossip and know it all with your colleague's personal life. It can be much harder to work with someone when you know the details of their personal life.
- You may also feel pressured to share details of your own personal life. A person with Autism may feel guarded about this and either not speak about it at all to reduce the risk of exposing any social and communication shortcomings or by creating a persona or fantasy world copying what you have seen and

heard from others. Honesty is the best policy here. Do not make up being in a relationship or your own fantasy family. Acknowledging your shortcomings and being honest about it is often appreciated by others and is more likely to win the respect of your colleagues.

- Be clear in your communications and always frame everything in the positive.
- Invest in an Autism (Neurodiversity) Coach outside of work to help you develop healthy boundaries between work and your personal life. Actively seek coaching on managing your finances as special interests and obsessions can lead to excessive spending and credit card debts.

Chapter Five

Lego®, minding your own business and more

In this chapter, I would like to share with you the issues of surviving and thriving as a working specialist Doctor with Autism. I will delve into how I used my passions and obsessions to help others. I will provide suggestions for setting up a workplace that is conducive to both the person with Autism and patient as well as tips for surviving day to day work stresses.

Teamwork, review meetings, morning teas, staff development forums, performance appraisals and various other organizational lingo (which I thought about as "mumbo jumbo" and dealing with other people) took an enormously long while for me to get used to and cope with. Any of those activities were almost always accompanied by a sense of dread, a knotted surge of anxiety and the inevitable headache.

In most settings, doctors must work within a multidisciplinary team. This is also the case in most non-medical settings, especially if you must deal with clients. I frequently had to ask myself, "Who Am I" as there were numerous covert dynamics, different personality traits and job descriptions within the team. There was even some overlap, particularly in Psychiatry with non-doctors within the team. A few of my medical colleagues were referring to their patients as clients and other non-doctors were referring to their clients as patients. This seemed like a trivial issue, but it was one that led me to question my identity as a doctor working within the field of Psychiatry.

In addition to this, there was the issue of Operational Leadership vs Clinical Leadership. I was taught that the former referred to the day to day management practices such as would occur within a hospital system. For example, the budget, the building and so on. Clinical leadership referred to taking direction in the clinical management of a patient. In other words, management refers to the process of achieving organizational goals by planning, organising, leading and controlling. Leadership on the other hand is the process of influencing others to engage in work behaviours necessary to reach organizational goals. I found the concept of these two different hierarchies quite confusing. I believed that they were not mutually exclusive. This difficulty was magnified in community mental health services where I worked as a Psychiatrist. There were many non-medical roles that I engaged in that would fall under the realm of Social Work in General Medicine. For example, exploring accommodation options for a homeless adolescent and liaising with employment agencies.

I realised that doctors are not trained to be managers. I should also emphasise that doctors with Autism most likely do not possess the natural skills to be managers. This is simply because it involves planning, organising, leading and managing people. Those who are obsessional and meticulously organised may excel in some aspects of management but without the necessary training and support are unlikely to succeed in leading and controlling people. Persons with Autism tend to be rules governed and black and white in their style of thinking. I was no exception and I should have remembered this when I was outvoted in school as the classroom monitor. Things had to be done by the book. I was often referred to as pedantic and meticulous, particularly by the administrative support staff and other colleagues. I was impatient when a team member worked too slowly and frustrated when the skill level was not up to my expectations.

Working within teams and becoming a successful Team Player requires several additional skills that may not come easily to the person with Autism. These include:

- Communication (verbal and nonverbal)
- Dealing with authority
- Coping with change
- Managing conflict
- Dealing with office politics
- Multitasking, organising and planning
- Flexibility and adaptability
- Accepting feedback, dealing with personal criticism and being wrong within a team meeting
- Putting differences aside for the sake of team stability
- Tolerating uncertainty regarding the competence of fellow team members
- Dealing with harassment and intimidation
- Accepting weaknesses and imperfection

It was a stressful journey as I slowly learned indirectly from observation and feedback that effective teamwork required agreed goals, an agreed approach, effective communication styles, established rules which guided interpersonal behaviours within the team, clear roles for each team member and competent leadership.

While I struggled with each of those, the strategies that eventually worked for me were:

- Regarding my colleagues with compassion and unconditional acceptance
- Consistently asking myself what it would be like in their shoes to bolster my empathy
- Releasing the pressure to change other people and instead focus on increasing their choices
- Listing down the strengths of a particular individual that I struggled to work with and mapping out visually how this fitted with the organizational strengths
- Learning and accepting the difference between leading and managing others with a focus on the leading component
- Setting limits to what I can and cannot do by being able to say no without feeling ashamed or guilty
- Fuelling my intellectual appetite by considering any setbacks as an opportunity to learn

- Believing that taking responsibility for others will only lead to further loss of control. I could only be responsible for myself.

Psychiatry as a medical specialty entails dealing with people on a day to day basis. You need to get to know a person in depth. Extensive "research" is required to understand the person within their context and the human condition. I came across several concepts used in the field of research that were very helpful to me in framing my journey as a person with Autism to acquire more knowledge about other people. I will now share this with you. Please indulge me as I expand on several research concepts. If this section does not resonate with you, do skip ahead to the summary two pages further along.

Paradigms are the theoretical mindsets or collections of beliefs that provide a way of thinking about the world. This underlined my approach towards regarding other people. Power relationships and action relationships are inherent in paradigms and this was particularly evident working in a team. A discourse refers to the meaning and power of language between people. In interactions with others, there is a dominant discourse and challenging discourses that arise from contrasting mindsets. I came across this daily in meetings within the work organization and with other organizations such as schools.

As an example, in the area of Autism, a dominant discourse is that it is pitiable to have a disability and sympathy is extended to the individual and family. An enactment of this discourse is the creation of respite services. The challenging discourse is that individuals with Autism are no different and should be treated just like any other member of the population. Therefore, I worked to support a paradigm shift from individuals seen as a burden to those with strengths and challenges. However, I discovered that entrenched mindsets were difficult to change let alone eradicate so there was still a significant level of stigma and discrimination present especially in individuals with Autism and mental illness who appear physically normal.

Ontology refers to a set of beliefs about reality and the nature of what the truth is. There are two types on which I shall elaborate. The first is *realism* in which one truth exists, the truth does not change, the truth can be discovered using objective measurements and this truth can be generalised to other situations once you find out what the truth is. The second type of ontology is the opposite view of realism known as *relativism*. In this view, there are multiple versions of reality. The truth is shaped by the context. It evolves and changes and cannot be transferred between contexts.

Epistemology relates to how we construct our beliefs about knowledge and how we come to know something. It considers relationships the researcher has with the research and the strategies for justifying beliefs. What the researcher believes about the nature of reality will dictate what level of relationship the researcher should have with whatever is being studied. There are researchers who believe that research should be done objectively. The researcher does not influence the data that is being gathered. The researcher needs to stay as far away as possible from the research by looking from the outside in to discover the truth. Examples include family observations. This is known as an etic epistemological approach. Realism leads to an etic epistemology.

On the other hand, there are researchers who believe that research should be done subjectively by looking from within. This involves interacting with people to find out what the truth means to them. The potential influence of the researcher on what is being researched may be acknowledged, avoided or even embraced. Examples include in depth psychiatric interviews. This is known as an emic epistemological approach. Relativism leads to an emic epistemology.

Methodologies are discipline specific approaches and processes of research. It incorporates both the theory and analytical processes that guide research. They can be divided based on the ontological and epistemological beliefs that led to them. For example, in an experimental methodology where experiments are designed to discover the truth, a realist ontological and etic epistemological approach is used. Methods are the specific ways for collecting research data such as an experiment to prove a cause. An experiment will also use a deductive approach to analysis. Data may be gathered from the results of blood tests and brain imaging to demonstrate responses to a specific treatment.

In a phenomenological study of lived experiences, a relativist ontology and emic epistemological approach are used. The methods may include in depth interviews, surveys and questionnaires. This enables as much information as possible to be gathered about a situation. Patterns are identified in the data. A tentative hypothesis is made, and more research undertaken to develop the conclusions. The results are always linked to the context. Research design decisions are made based on complex philosophies about how data is collected and analysed. This is an inductive approach to analysis.

In summary, I have elaborated on these concepts in my Autism journey as a working professional as I feel it is very relevant in how we develop our social and emotional skills in the workplace. We need to take on the role of a researcher who is active at times and passive in others. We learn by observation and some of us will feel safer using the outsider/objective approach. However, to be more in touch with the human condition and to develop more empathy, we need to also be able to take the insider/subjective approach. Therefore, it is not an *either or* but a *both and* approach that we need to take. To be a skilful working adult with Autism, the ontology, epistemology, methodology and methods used need to be flexible and adaptable.

Although I never considered this perspective until very recently, my Resume was really a jointly (and unconsciously) developed treatment program between myself and the field of Psychiatry to learn the required life skills to survive as a working adult with Autism. I gained experiences that I never did as a child. It gave me an opportunity to relive my childhood on different terms. Training as a Psychiatrist taught me many people skills that I lacked earlier on. The skills that I learned were then used not just for my own personal benefit but for the service of patients, students and the wider community. I believe the relevant psychological terms for these actions are *sublimation and altruism* which I now recognise as two of my core strengths as a person with Autism.

Despite the challenges of being an undiagnosed doctor with Autism, I am still grateful to the various supervisors that I had who showed me very professional ways of communicating with other people and using humour to deal with workplace, communication and organizational challenges.

Specific examples of my training that provided invaluable experiences for my Autism journey were:

- Deescalating agitated patients using crisis intervention interviewing skills with restraint only as a last resort (communication skills, dealing with meltdowns)
- Developing and collecting clinical information verbally and in writing with structured Clinical Assessment Schedules (communication and organizational skills)
- Developing and delivering formal teaching programs to senior medical students face to face and through Video Conferencing (communication and improving empathic attunement)
- Understanding the whole person using a bio-psycho-social-spiritual-cultural assessment approach particularly with Aboriginal people, migrants and refugees from the Eastern Mediterranean Region (improving empathic attunement)
- Networking and partnerships with other medical and non-medical health professionals, Non-Government Organizations and private practitioners. For example, Developmental Physicians, Educational Psychologists, Private Speech Pathologists, Private Occupational Therapists, Neurologists, Sleep

Physicians and Cardiologists (communication skills, making and keeping friends)
- Training in specific forms of psychological therapy such as Cognitive Behaviour Therapy, Group Therapy and Family Therapy (my own therapy to overcome anxiety and depression)
- Managing inpatient dynamics between patients and staff and between staff members. This included management of staff conflict and critical incidents (managing workplace politics and bullying)
- Use of Telemedicine to provide consultation to General Practitioners and rural clinicians regarding appropriateness of referrals, immediate risk management and long-term care (improved verbal communication skills with less pressure needed on the nonverbal component)
- Initiating weekly trainee doctor morale boosting meetings to promote voice, choice and feedback to the Senior Consultant body (improving self-esteem)
- Advocacy for the safety of doctors working in the Emergency Department and coordinating meetings with the relevant stakeholders to design an interview

room setting more conducive to psychiatric interviewing (working with change and dealing with sensory issues)
- Supervising junior and senior trainees (improving self-esteem and empathic attunement)
- Participating as role player in clinical examinations (adopting a different persona or "faking it")
- Convening a Peer Review Group comprising Psychiatrists and Consultant Physicians (making and keeping friends).

As the years progressed in public practice, working days seemed to be filled with Case meetings, Team Meetings, Business Meetings and Staff Development Meetings. There seemed to be less and less time for seeing patients. There was an enormous amount of pressure to complete computer statistics to demonstrate time spent in various work activities. Humour remained an important survival mechanism during this time and I decided not to attend a meeting unless "it was funny". The Staff Development meetings were hilarious, particularly with one particular presenter who was focused on ergonomics, posture and movement. Inevitably, there was a regression to toilet humour and bottoms.

I discovered that I needed more time and energy to prepare for meetings and if possible, review a written agenda beforehand. Not only did this allay my Autistic anxieties by providing structure, it also allowed a clear set of actionable steps to be taken after meetings. It was very easy to slip into a "you vs me" mentality in group meetings which was heightened by the Autistic tendency towards black and white (all or nothing) thinking. My advice is to resist this and remember that what is in the group or organization's best interest is of paramount consideration. A mutual set of actionable steps should be documented and circulated to all parties with a review date set for accountability.

I found it challenging to leave the safer office environment and go out for meetings and any community events. I am sure that many doctors would rather spend time in their clinics seeing patient after patient. It is important to consider what the purpose of the meeting is, whether it is necessary and obtain the perspective of others. It is always important to check beforehand whether alternative means of attendance or contribution can work just as well so that you can be adequately prepared to enter a potentially confronting social situation and not stress yourself unnecessarily.

Despite these self-management attempts, there were still numerous challenges that eventually led to an enormous amount of stress on myself and the growing frustrations working within the public system. The statistics continued to be alarming. Worldwide, up to 20% of young adults suffer from a disabling mental illness. Suicide is a leading cause of death among adolescents and Major Depressive Disorder often has its onset in adolescence. There was much talk about the preventative aspect of care but the system I was working in was very much acute/crisis driven.

I was also faced with several moral and ethical dilemmas associated with:

- Labelling children and adults with a disorder for the sake of resource allocation (funding) for services
- The widespread use of psychotropic medications despite its limitations in chronic symptom management
- The uncertainties about the long-term effects of medications and medicating the individual person for the sake of the family and wider system

- Scapegoating of the child or individual person when the problem was with the adult or wider system
- Burden of dealing with chronic health or lifestyle problems and not just disorders
- The push for evidence-based medicine with no new major discoveries to advance treatments in psychiatry

Unfortunately, I was gradually ensnared in an intolerable paradox. There was a strong sense of apathy mixed with deep feelings of shame and guilt. I became quite depressed. Ultimately, this led to my resignation from public practice. I decided to go out on my own and discover what it would be like to set up a business to make a unique type of difference to the lives of the patients, carers and their families.

One of the first ambitions I had early in my working life was having my own place in which I could help others in my own terms. I became very focused on the intricacies of setting up my own practice. I chose a large sized office which was on the first floor and away from the hustle and bustle of traffic. Each room was designed for a specific purpose. There was a main consulting room, a group room, a medical room, a waiting room and a closed off reception area. I also designed a small room as a quiet area for myself.

It was a place in which I could withdraw, lie down and have a break.

I must have pushed the fitout technicians to their limit. The doors had to be installed perfectly straight, the paint perfectly textured, the walls adequately soundproofed, and the electrical outlets precisely positioned. It was a very stressful time dealing with the painters, plumbers, electricians and cabinet makers. The heightened anxiety increased my obsessive-compulsive tendencies and I survived the period after appointing my father (who was an Engineer) to oversee the building works and interact with the workers. I now understand that he would have found this extremely stressful as well given his autistic tendencies, but the end product was well worth it as it not only became a clinic designed for a doctor with Autism but also his patients with Autism.

It was during this time that my passion for Lego® re-emerged and a Lego® themed clinic that would appeal to all ages was created. I became an Adult Fan of Lego® (AFOL). It was not easy to fit in my own obsession with Lego® with the other demands of clinical practice such as report writing and seeing patients about "non-Lego®" matters. This illustration however is an example of how an Autism special interest can be used in your work as a means of engaging with others and in setting up an appealing work environment. Moreover, it gives the person with Autism a safe opportunity to use his special interest to build on his ability to read nonverbal cues.

Lego®

I found it difficult to strike a balance between developing a clinically appealing environment and not turn it into a cluttered toyshop or Lego® wonderland. I recall a girl who would empty out all the Lego® bricks in the tubs in the waiting room and pretend to swim in it backwards, forwards and sideways. We also had to be careful about disabled individuals mouthing the Lego® and pet dogs swallowing the bricks. I had an Electrolux steam cleaner to sanitise the Lego® (not as regularly as I would have preferred).

I relied heavily on my staff (and father) to assist with the setup, cleaning and repair of Lego® sets. Broken sets were inevitable given the fragile nature of Lego® to touch. I am sure the ladies at the front desk required more than a few drinks after work to recalibrate after frantically building and repairing Lego® for the day. I shall be forever grateful to them and my father for their patience and willingness to venture beyond the box to help the patients. In hindsight, if I had formally known that I was on the Autism Spectrum, I would have had a frank discussion with them (with the support of a Psychologist) on how to handle a demanding boss with Autism. I would have also employed a person with the title "Lego Executive Assistant" for the clinic.

Within the clinic, several "Lego Zones" were established to cater for different stages of development ranging from toddlers to adults. In addition to chronological age, anyone who was interested in Lego® was also classed into Lego® developmental stages from apprentice to builders to true masters who had photographic memories of instructions and buildings.

For the under 6s, Lego® Duplo was a firm favourite. These large sized bricks are easier to hold and click in place. It was less taxing to visually scan for the right brick to fit into the right place. I highly recommend Duplo trains with sound effects. Colourful pieces of furniture, doors, windows, roofs, flowers, fruits and animals are essential for creative building. Children (and adults) can also build towers up to the ceiling (with assistance to hold it up) and join together several base plates of what they build. This is usually a representation of their home, school and family (either actual or perceived). A picture of their creations to take home is also a must to highlight their achievement.

For the 6s to 12s, Lego® City and its variations are best for those who prefer structured building. It is important to keep up to date with the contemporary sets such as Star Wars, Ninjago, Marvel Superheroes and Friends. I was particularly pleased with the Friends series which catered for the girls and women (and boys and men). It provided a detailed and colourful addition to the Lego® scene. For those who like to free build houses (homes) and cities, having all the traditional Lego® bricks on hand is necessary to allow freedom of expression. Lego® City trains were another firm favourite. The toy sections of the big departmental stores hold regular sales. Assortments of used Lego® can also be found online through sites such as Gumtree as a cheaper alternative. The Lego® should be steam cleaned regularly to prevent cross contamination of germs. This may be an issue for the Autism doctor with OCD (Obsessive Compulsive Disorder) and compulsive cleaning. A pocket-sized hand sanitiser was my saving grace.

More Lego®

Adolescents often lose interest as they graduate from the "Golden Age of Lego". For those who remain interested, Lego® Technic is a must. The doctor with Autism can be an excellent builder and fixer of Lego® Technic (provided that soft motor skills are not a difficulty). Examples include cranes, trucks and planes with hydraulic pumps, pulleys and battery-operated motors. I remember several patients who could fix the Lego® without referring to the instructions and immediately spot a part that was out of place.

There were also numerous adult patients interested in Lego®. Most of them were from an Architectural background or simply had their passion rekindled because of their child. For these adults, Lego® Technic, the Lego® Architecture Series and the Ultimate Collectors Editions such as the Death Star, Millennium Falcon, Batmobile and Superstar Destroyer should be a welcome addition (without becoming a distraction) to any serious conversational topic about health and mental illness.

I spent quite some time observing how my patients (regardless of age) interacted with Lego®. I was not aware of this at the time, but it was an opportunity for me to step back, have a brain break and picture things from above like a bird. It gave me great insight into their inner world and assisted with the assessment and diagnostic formulation. Things I noted included distractibility, choice of theme, ability to manage frustration and delay gratification. The number of careless errors when following instructions, ability to free build, amount of fidgeting, need for movement to focus and choice to build alone or with collaborators provided invaluable information about the whole person. Indeed, I often referred to this as a Lego® State Examination in as much as I viewed the state of my patient's dentition as a Dental State Examination.

At this point, I would like to share with you how a special interest can be used to develop fundamental social skills for any person on the Autism Spectrum. I will use the example of an educational environment as it worked very well but it was also successful in an adult working environment such as an Architecture firm. In the same manner, a workplace Lego® group for staff morale and social skills building with the Autism employee has the potential to be very effective.

In this example, I managed to persuade several schools to implement a "Lego Development Group" for social skills building during the lunch period. I invited the Principal or Deputy Principal and Learning Support Coordinator of those schools to visit my clinic for inspiration. I firmly believed it important for school staff to shift their mentality about children who are internalisers or introverts. Extroverts recharge from social interactions. Introverts and those with Autism recharge by solitude. They would rather not spend time kicking the football (Aussie Footie) in the playground but instead undertake a quiet indoor activity.

Each "Lego Development Group" or Club had up to 10 students and two staff members. They included children with Autism and Anxiety. These groups were facilitated by staff who had knowledge on how to build Lego®. I encouraged Teachers to read about the history of Lego®, the cult of Lego® and survey Lego® catalogues for additional ideas. I provided them with Lego® Magazines for additional information. It was essential for staff to receive a level of Lego® training to enable them to connect genuinely with their students. If they did not know much about it, they should be prepared to learn from their students. There is also a significant difference between building Lego® from the imagination and from instructions. Persons with Autism often require a more structured and predictable approach in the first instance. Once they feel more secure and comfortable within the group dynamic, free association and building from the imagination can then occur spontaneously.

Each school term, one child was designated the Lego® Expert and an opportunity was given for another child to be the Expert or Mentor the following term. Turns were also taken to find the pieces, read the instructions and build. Lego® became a powerful motivator that significantly assisted with the day to day behavioural support of a child with Autism. In addition, sharing, valuing the contributions and constructions of others, negotiating for parts and projects were other skills that they developed. Thus, the fundamental social skills for any person on the Autism Spectrum were naturally practiced in a pleasurable group setting. It was also invaluable to have teachers who knew the background of the students involved in the groups. They needed to see what those children were like outside the classroom environment.

It was critical for them to "get their hands dirty", build with the bricks, and model appropriate frustration and conflict resolution themselves.

Specific Lego® Club rules included, "if you break it, you have to fix it. If you can't fix it, ask for help. If someone else is using it, don't take it, ask first. No yelling. Use inside voices. No climbing or jumping on the furniture. No teasing, name calling or bullying. No hitting or wrestling. Keep your hands and feet to yourself. Clean up and put things back where they belong". These rules were presented as pictures and words. Lego® points were awarded for pro-social and Lego® related achievements. These could be traded in for Lego® prizes.

There were practical difficulties. It was not possible to run groups more than once a week because of competing staff priorities. Teachers on recess duty had to supervise up to 100 students in each playground. When they were taken out to work with 10 students in the Club, it placed pressure on other staff to increase the amount of supervision required of the other students. Getting staff to miss their lunch was not a good idea. Lego® was also expensive. Finding the appropriate space to construct as well as an area to display

Lego® safely without the risk of being torn apart by unexpected visitors was challenging. Any difficulties should not however deter the doctor with Autism from being creative and pursuing the use of an Autism strength (such as Lego®) to build confidence and self-esteem.

A frequent issue I faced as the person who "makes the diagnosis" was the notion from either staff or family that the person is fine in their environment so there cannot be a problem. For example, when the child misbehaves at home but is fine in school and vice versa. The doctor with Autism's thoughts can get stuck on the issue of why people do not understand mental illness and how invisible it can be, especially when a person is out of their comfort zone. I often mentally rehearsed my responses to this question over and over in my office or car. This can create unnecessary stress, anxiety, physical and mental tension. In this situation, it is important to educate staff and family about the nature of mental illness and adopt the stance of preventative care. This can be conveyed in writing or presented in person pre-emptively. I imagined my eyes peering through a telescope. Sometimes I needed to zoom in and at other times I needed to zoom out to see the bigger picture and not dwell on minutiae. The flexible role of a Researcher who can base approach to context as I outlined earlier in this chapter was also useful.

I should note at this point the differences between working with primary schools and high schools. This would similarly apply to working in large vs small organizations. In primary school, you deal with the Teacher (or two if they job shared), the School Psychologist, Learning Support Coordinator, Deputy Principal/Principal. In high school, the number of people you need to deal with rises exponentially, as each subject has a different Teacher. This mirrors the sense of being overwhelmed that students and parents experience when they transition to high school, particularly if they too are on the Autism spectrum. In this instance, a higher level of organization is required to either meet with as many Teachers as early as possible before the start of classes or to have a designated person in school collate and distribute all the information.

Dealing with multiple lines of thought is energy depleting for the person with Autism. There may be a dominant discourse with multiple challenging discourses. I accepted that making an attempt at exchange of information is better than not having one at all. An A4 page summarizing the issues of the student, their strengths and adjustments required, prepared collaboratively live and online with the School Psychologist or Learning Support Coordinator (for example through Google Docs) was the best compromise.

It was true for me that some of the characteristics of Autism become more prominent with age. A particular issue was my adversity to the sensory demands of any environment. Perhaps the energies and pace of offices and businesses or organizational spaces have also changed over the course of time. It reactivated my past experiences of sensory overload in school as a child. On this matter, the doctor with Autism should have a visual sensory thermometer in place to gauge before and after entering a "sensorily" aversive environment. This includes the Emergency Department. Once this scale hits an 8 (when sounds start to echo in the head or the ears start to ring), it is time to have a sensory break and if feasible, consider technology as an alternative to face to face attendance.

As rewarding as private practice was with the satisfaction of seeing patients actually getting better consistently and the big boost that this had to my sense of self, I failed to recognise that I was still getting more and more stressed with increased anxiety and sleeplessness. Seeing patient after patient without a break was taking its toll. Another important sign of decompensation was a change in my attitude towards new patient queries and my staff. I became increasingly rigid in who I should be seeing, charged fees for even responding to a phone call and turned away many new patients particularly if they had signs of Autism. I also became very strict with the expected behaviour of current patients. Anyone who missed more than three appointments in a row or whom I did not see for six months would be automatically discharged. My staff would have noticed that I was becoming increasingly rigid and inflexible with my boundaries. I was relating to them more as objects rather than people.

In the end, I ended up being married to my work. Any human connections I had were with my patients and I had no personal life to speak of. If I had to draw a Wheel of Life which included relationships outside of work, finances, having my own family, recreational pursuits and satisfaction with life, this wheel would be quite flat. After a period of becoming less Autistic and connected with others, I was entering a phase of my life where I was becoming more Autistic with age and work experience.

It was fortunate that I went down the route of supplements which I always advocated for my patients prior to commencing psychotropic medications. These certainly helped me:

- Magnesium for its calming effects on the nervous system
- Vitamin D for calcium absorption, bone health and cognitive functioning
- Zinc for brain development and sensory processing
- Essential Omega-3 Fatty Acids for cellular, immune function, hair and skin health.
- Probiotics
- Multivitamin supplement
- Gluten, casein and soy free diet

I suggest you consider giving these a good go as part of your own self-care program as a doctor with Autism.

Other top tips:

- Setting up your own business or practice is extremely hard work. While it may be very appealing to go out on your own to avoid the stress of dealing with other personalities at work, it can be a recipe for emotional exhaustion and burnout. It is important to have at least weekly check ins with a Mentor or Coach and set up blocks to your weekly schedule for different types of work activities. Block out consistent times for a sensory break and nourishment each day.
- Do not underestimate the effects of physical and mental clutter on your mental health. I overindulged, obsessed and filled my workplace with too much Lego ® and unnecessary clutter. I should have researched online examples of a simple and friendly environment for my senses.
- Helping others is as much an Art as it is a Science. The art of diplomacy is crucial when working within a team and external agencies. This skill does not come easily to the doctor with Autism. It can be very exhausting balancing multiple human and non-human

agendas. Avoid the urge to do everything yourself in order to feel in control. Delegate to other professionals. Remember that less is often more.
- Accept that there will be people who just *do not get* Autism and mental health. You can explain until you are "blue in the face" and yet they do not understand. Resist the urge to change anyone not following your rules. They are responsible for themselves. Remind yourself to let these people go at the end of each day and to start each day afresh.
- You can have very high expectations of yourself and others. The expectations that you set of others can come across in social interactions as critical, cold and condescending. Have a post it note next to your computer screen to never judge people and always view them with Curiosity and Compassion. Write C and C on the back of your hand.
- It is easy to get stuck on negative thoughts and feelings when analysing verbal and nonverbal cues from others. Avoid energy draining and look for energy giving activities. As much as you can, hold the most

positive vision for your patients in all areas of their lives.

- To be a skilled professional with Autism, you must learn to connect with your patients at the level of their interests. This often includes the need to do your own research on the latest video games, movies, You Tubers and social media channels. Avoid the temptation to launch into business talk all the time and engage in social chit chat to build a relationship first.

- Focus on the present while at work. Avoid the past which heightens depressive thinking and the future which increases anxiety. Take three deep breaths before each client and set an intention for how you would like to feel when each encounter is complete. Do not spend too much time mentally rehearsing what you have to say. Stop after a count of three.

- Have spring water (which is live water) on your table to keep yourself hydrated at one cup per hour. Note that elimination is just as important as intake. Do not forgo regular toilet breaks (at least 3 per working day). It is also deeply relaxing to shrug your shoulders,

rotate your neck, extend your lower back and stretch your quadriceps (hamstrings).
- Begin any meeting by celebrating successes and discuss something positive that is of interest to the patient. Always begin and conclude with a positive intention.
- Avoid engaging in a battle of wills with your patient.
- It is highly likely if you are seeing a patient with Autism that you will either end up talking at each other about individual interests or for one to end up simply smiling and nodding. Have a nonverbal cue on hand to remind yourself to stop and give the other person a turn. A set of communication cards can also work well when they contain simple phrases such as, "Thank you. It is my turn to speak now. I am sorry, but you are going off topic."
- As appealing as your special interest can be to build rapport with your patients, especially those with Autism, set boundaries to ensure that it does not become an obsession for yourself. There are dangers in being caught up with the detail and not "seeing the

wood for the trees". Ask regularly, "Is this for me, or my patient, or both?

- Do not underestimate the power of self-reflection. If you have your own office, invest in a recliner and prescribe for yourself 15 minutes quiet time in the middle of the day and 15 minutes after your last patient. Loosen your collar, belt and remove footwear. Wear an eye shade and noise cancelling headphones. Listen to a meditative exercise to calm your sympathetic nervous system.

- Embrace technology. Use your smartphone and video conferencing applications whenever possible and do not overload yourself with face to face interactions. Strike a balance between interacting in person and virtually for meetings. Focus on listening to the voice alone and you will find yourself feeling more refreshed and energetic despite a long working day. To avoid being distracted by applications on your phone, install and set an App blocker for your working hours.

- If you do have to go out of your office for a work meeting, have your Dictaphone or Smartphone on hand to record your mental notes before you drive off. This will prevent the details playing over and over in your head. These notes can be subsequently transcribed. It is OK to say no to sharing transport if there is discomfort with sharing an enclosed space.

- You will be constantly faced with the dilemma of whether you have done enough and how much more you could have done to help a particular person. Remember that individuals are responsible for themselves and you can be satisfied if you helped that person develop a range of choices in which they can make their own decisions.
- Do not underestimate the importance of Continuing Professional Development (CPD) with colleagues from a range of professional backgrounds. Individual supervision and even therapy may even be mandatory depending on your personal and professional circumstances.

Chapter Six
From Doctor to Patient

The following two chapters focus on the issue of survival and transformation for a doctor with Autism in the face of sudden change, life crisis and stigma. A reversal of roles can be difficult for any person, particularly a professional person with Autism. You never know when your life will change. It can happen gradually. It can happen suddenly. You may or may not be able to plan for it. Predictability is particularly important if you are on the Autism spectrum. Alas, life is not like that and no matter how meticulous I was in ensuring that my life was scheduled and planned in advance, in no way did I ever anticipate having a total breakdown. My worst nightmare in which I would lose control of my life became a reality.

I had always been obsessive compulsive since I was a child. Looking back, my life revolved around specific routines and rituals such as cleaning, praying, thinking a certain thought or magic number in my head over and over until it felt just right, walking across the pavement a certain way, positioning objects and checking under my school desk the right number of times until I felt it was safe to go home.

Back in those days, no one in Malaysia knew anything about OCD (Obsessive Compulsive Disorder) and as I still appeared to do well in school and was well behaved, it was not viewed as a problem. My parents and friends did enquire on occasions why I needed to keep checking things, clean the car and why my eyes rolled up and down but nothing further was looked into at the time.

The eye rolling habit I learnt later was a Tic, a semi voluntary twitch of a muscle or group of muscles. Other tics that I have experienced over time included grunting, sniffing, twitching my cheeks up and my jaw muscles from side to side. It was difficult to hide the tics at work. I did not realise how tiring it was to hold the muscles together and then have a big release in private between patients and after work, hoping that no one would see what I was up to.

Depression and anxiety tend to go hand in hand and that was likely to have been the case for me. I was becoming an automaton working day in day out. Life became even more isolatory and ritualistic. I worked harder and harder for the approval of my parents, especially my father and all the people whom I saw. I became obsessed about taking my parents away on big expensive holidays before they became too old to travel.

All these habits wore me out and even though I was still functioning well at work, I was pulled down by a pervasive sense of emptiness and a loss of pleasure in many things that I was doing. Despite the satisfaction I obtained from seeing people feeling happier, I felt that something was missing. I did not feel a whole sense of self. I began to question whether I was in the right career, whether I needed a dramatic change in direction, whether I was burnt out or whether I needed to approach my chosen profession from a different perspective.

It seemed that I was working because I had to rather than because I wanted to. I suppose that is the danger with using extrinsic goals for happiness like income, possessions, image and reputation. I also succumbed to lifestyle creep. The more I earned, the more I spent. People say that doctors are rich but that is not necessarily true. It is very easy for us to obtain finance and doctors I gather are often working excessively to finance multiple loans for their practices, homes, cars and investment properties.

I simply could not hold it together for much longer. It took hours for me to fall asleep each night and even then, my sleep was restless and fragmented. I constantly worried about what I had said and done the day before. I could not stop rehearsing in my mind over and over the things that I should be saying to various people the following day. I woke up in the early hours of the morning, tossed and turned without falling back asleep again. I did not realise it at the time but I was eating recklessly. I had two Up and Gos (breakfast drinks) and a bowl of instant cereal each morning while reviewing patient reports. I almost never found time for lunch and binged on dinner, again while reviewing reports and completing paperwork on the computer. I also developed a craving for sweet desserts and would consume a tub of my favourite vanilla ice cream and a bowlful of Taiwanese Dessert several nights a week. For those of you who do not know what this dessert is, it is a large version of Bubble Tea pearls with shaved ice, fruits, syrup and condensed milk. The amount of sugar that I was exposing myself to led to a roller coaster ride of sleeplessness, anxiety and mood swings. It was fortunate that I did not go down the path of alcohol, smoking and recreational drugs.

And then it happened. You cannot really describe a breakdown until you have personally experienced it. My mind was going at a million miles an hour. My thinking was jumbled. I could not sleep. I was petrified with anxiety. The compulsive rituals spiralled out of control. I had a constant knotted feeling in my chest. I could not breathe. I had to force myself to work and face everyone. I wished that I was dead and had distressing thoughts about how I could end my life as well as intrusive images of death. My senses were tuned up by 1000%. Every single breath, footsteps and rustle hurt my ears. Light became overly intense and I was acutely sensitive to smells. I should note that persons with Autism are particularly prone to anxiety, depression and suicide attacks.

At this point, I should talk about suicide in professionals. According to the latest statistics from the Centre for Disease Control in the USA, Doctors, Dentists and Health Care Professionals are ranked as 19 on the list of highest suicide occupations. Other notable professions that are likely to include Autism individuals are Engineers (ranked 5), Computer Programmers, Mathematicians and Statisticians (ranked 8), Scientists and Lab Technicians (ranked 13)

Accountants (ranked 14), Nursing, Medical Assistants and Health Care Support Workers (ranked 15), Office Workers and Administrative Support Workers (ranked 21) and Librarians (ranked 22).

Therefore, there are a significant number of professions that persons with Autism appear to be more vulnerable to in terms of suicide. The reasons behind these are not clear but if you happen to be working in any one of them, please be mindful of these thoughts and speak to a trusted person or professional about them as soon as possible. These thoughts need to have a safe outlet before they become dangerous to yourself or others. The other risk factors include male gender, a history of depression, self-harm, attempted suicide, alcohol abuse, social isolation and recent life crisis. I think it is also highly important for people already working in these professions at risk to talk to their trainees and interns about this real risk of suicide and make sure that pathways are available for ongoing support.

It is important to distinguish between passive ideas of dying and suicidal thoughts. I experienced the former during periods of heightened stress and anxiety, thinking that life was too hard and what the point was. They became suicidal thoughts after my breakdown when I actively thought of how I could end my life. Any thoughts of dying need to be taken seriously as the risk to yourself will increase when they become more intense and frequent.

As for me, I had not seen my General Practitioner for a year and the last visit was for an insurance examination. It is likely that professionals with Autism, especially those in the health professions do not see their own doctor regularly for surveillance. A referral was completed for me to see a private Psychiatrist. It was not possible for me to find a Psychiatrist who had a special interest in Autism. I was fortunate to have one that was open to further investigation. I considered myself lucky that I still had the financial resources to see a private practitioner as the shame and waiting periods in the public system would have been much more difficult to bear. It is quite likely that I would be given up on my plans to see anyone. I also felt embarrassed, humiliated and ashamed at having to stop work so suddenly and to have let so many people down. This led to crippling anxiety, nightmares and panic attacks.

I was soon diagnosed with severe Depression, Obsessive-Compulsive Disorder, Post Traumatic Stress and a Tic

Disorder. I was referred to an Autism Specialist for further testing. I was started on several medications. Fluvoxamine for depression and OCD (Obsessive Compulsive Disorder), Quetiapine for sleep, Lamotrigine as an add on for depression, Vitamin D for depression and high strength Fish Oil for depression and anxiety. I was referred to a Psychologist for talking therapy. I was advised that it would take time for me to get better and that I needed to take a complete sabbatical from work.

I was dumbfounded and questioned myself repeatedly why I had not seen it coming and sought help earlier. After all, I planned so well for everything else. It would seem that I was completely blind to my own needs. As a doctor, I was certainly not a good patient. Perhaps my introverted personality played a part. Perhaps a certain degree of pride and arrogance that I was invincible. I was reminded that mental illness is very invisible, and it can creep up insidiously when you least expect it. I tried to console myself in this way. I tried not to judge and blame myself but it was easier said than done. There was a voice in my head that kept telling me what a bad person I was, that I ought to be ashamed of myself, that I was useless and worthless. I felt angry, guilty, disappointed, sad and shameful all at once.

The formal diagnosis of Autism finally made sense to many struggles that I had experienced in my life. I was relieved and yet disappointed with myself that I had not discovered it sooner. I was so focussed on helping others that I was also blind to the fact that I have Autism. I was baffled as to why none of my colleagues who knew me so well ever suggested or even implied that I was on the Autism spectrum and that a diagnosis may have been useful at the very least for my own awareness. As a working professional with Autism, you can be successful and appear to function well on the surface because you have learnt to skilfully camouflage your symptoms in the eyes of others.

It was a miracle that I survived those dark months of my life. I am quite certain I came close to suicide but for some reason I survived. Just as suddenly as the breakdown had occurred, I gradually began to experience a breakthrough. The top three things that pulled me through that period was my firm belief that I could still make positive choices and take responsibility for myself, a few family members and friends who gave their unconditional support and self-help which I will share with you as you read on into the next chapter. Perhaps it was all fated. Perhaps it was also my belief in the powers of Autism and the unwavering faith of my family in the universe that all will be well.

Here it is important to point out the tendency of the Autism mind to ruminate over and analyse in detail everything that happens to you. It is like a track in Repeat 1 mode. Instead, you should tell yourself that any feelings of frustration, sadness, anger and despair can be replaced with a sense of curiosity and compassion towards yourself. Your thoughts may keep veering towards the negative. When it happens, say to yourself, "What can I still choose to do now that will make today 1% better?"

You should however never underestimate the resilience that Autism can give you. Whether or not you are diagnosed, the persistence and determination that has brought you to where you are now as a professional, how well you have coped with the social, sensory and emotional challenges has in fact tuned your body to withstand many of life's ongoing challenges. You are probably going to cope with what is ahead of you better than you ever imagined.

I struggled to gain acceptance from others that I was mentally ill. Despite efforts to destigmatise mental illness, the campaigns and the reforms for which I say that some progress has been made, there is still a large amount of stigma, particularly for those individuals who appear normal. People have a natural tendency to judge. I believe that it is those who often appear the least disabled in the eyes of others who often need a lot more emotional and social support. These two areas are the most crucial for a person with Autism, particularly if you have been diagnosed with Asperger's Syndrome, High Functioning Autism or Level 1 Autism. It is the small things in life that often turn out to be the very big things for us.

I was grateful to have received kind words of support and acts of generosity from others. This included a friend visiting once a week, a relative bringing lunch, work colleagues and patients sending get well cards. As important as those acts were for my recovery, I also came to accept that I would be waiting a long time for things to change if I relied on others and for anyone to understand me fully. I needed to get out of a "disabled", "I cannot do it now" and victim mindset.

I realised that acceptance from others was secondary to acceptance of myself. I needed to slow down, connect at a deeper level with my environment and form positive relationships with people outside of work. This is easier said than done for a person with Autism as the tendency is to relate to objects, withdraw into a world of your own or participate in social interactions on your own terms.

I had almost forgotten that I learnt piano for 8 years as a child and realised that I should reframe my approach towards choosing or modifying my career using the intrinsic skills that I obtained as a child whilst learning a musical instrument. It was important for me to listen to feedback from my peers and colleagues and to acknowledge that failure is part of the journey which I now must take to achieve progress. I admitted that I made a mistake in putting work ahead of my health and not recognising that I can achieve just as much by doing less.

I needed to widen my network by meeting with others regularly and not work in isolation all the time. I came to realise and accept that it was not going to be easy to change the way that I had operated for such a long time. It was almost like I needed to learn to become unstuck and have a fresh and creative take on life. I sold my home to settle my debts. This meant that I lost my own space which is very crucial for anyone with Autism. Having my own home previously meant I had achieved independence and could develop a sensorily friendly environment. Everything was just right from an OCD (Obsessive Compulsive Disorder) point of view. My obsessions were symmetrically displayed. My cars were my family. My work was my family. My home was my safe zone. I lost all these in a short space of time. Never in my life did I feel so lost and alone. I moved in with my parents and although it has not been an easy experience, I am very grateful to them for taking me in and putting up with my eccentricities.

I became quite concerned about the effect of medications. There was no doubt that they were helpful in my recovery, but I came to appreciate that they are only a band aid, providing important initial relief of symptoms during the acute period. I experienced significant side effects such as shaking, restlessness, persistent tiredness and impaired short-term memory. I felt numb and slowed down. I could not smile. I could not laugh. This was not the way that I wanted to be. I finally understood what it was like for my patients to have experienced side effects from medications that I used to prescribe. It filled me with feelings of guilt and shame. I was however consoled by the knowledge that I never prescribed medications on its own and used the metaphor, "Medications can only help you stop and think. They help the other treatments work more effectively so that you can make better choices for yourself." I realised that I needed to look at other ways to enable a sustained recovery, address the chronic issues and consider which treatment option was best for me in the longer term.

There are dangers to a doctor self-diagnosing and treating. This includes prescribing tablets for anxiety and sleep. It may seem convenient at the outset but you enter a slippery slope in which you lose sight of who the patient is and any form of accountability for your actions. Unless it is a simple physical ailment, it is particularly important for any doctor to avoid diagnosing and prescribing any medications for themselves.

It is crucial during crisis for the Autism mind to remain intellectually stimulated. You should avoid at all costs the tendency to sit around like a vegetable. You must do all you can to fight any apathy and loss of motivation. It is important to have a continuing life mission, remove yourself from any feelings of self-importance and attachment to your own ego. Think of this as a time in which your brain will need to complete a software reinstall and not just an update. You will need to give your brain time to unlearn all that it has learnt and rewire itself.

An important issue to deal with during this time is the relationship that you have with those living at home with you. This may be your partner, your children, your siblings, a house mate and more likely than not your parents and grandparents. There are challenges with sharing a home for someone with Autism, particularly if there are other family members with Autism, whether diagnosed or not. One of the constants in life is that there will be problems. There will be situations or people that annoy the person with Autism. As a professional, you may still find yourself in an entwined relationship with your parents or loved one. There may be an imbalance between care and control. This can stifle creativity, individuality and independence. It can negatively affect how you form relationships with other people. It is easy to constantly judge and criticise your parents and loved ones.

In order to form positive relationships with others as a person with Autism, you need to release your attachment to any outcomes and adopt the stance of working with the person rather than against them to facilitate change. Practise listening to their point of view. This will not come naturally for a person with Autism as the tendency is to focus on yourself. I needed to accept the things in a relationship that I could not change and work on those that I could.

A bonsai gift from my uncle signifying peace, balance and connection with nature

Chapter Seven
The Road to Recovery

Through my own online and offline research, I developed a self-help programme to rehabilitate my lifestyle factors. It was a deeply humbling experience to have to sit in the patient's chair and receive advice from other professionals for a change. It was a steep learning curve indeed. I brought a treatment journal with me to make notes of what had transpired in each session. Whilst they provided useful tips, it was very expensive, particularly when I was at the stage of weekly appointments. I realised that it was up to me to take their advice on board and develop my own Autism recovery plan which consisted of the following steps:

1) Decluttering, letting go of obsessions and extrinsic goals of happiness

You may be a successful doctor or other professional who has a big home with the latest smart technology, a farm that you can go to on the weekends, a fleet of cars and a top reputation. All these perpetuate a sense of self-importance. These possessions are extrinsic to yourself. I realised how fleeting they were when I lost them so quickly in a flash of time. Nothing in life is free. If you have less of one, there will be more of another. Trade in many (I am not necessarily saying all) these things for intrinsic goals of happiness such as love of self, safety and belonging.

Begin by decluttering your wallet. Discard receipts and cards that you no longer need. Make it simple and light. Declutter your office desk. Throw away any unused drawer items. Give away used journals and magazines. Declutter your bedroom and wardrobe. Donate clothes and shoes that you only use once or twice a year. Declutter your bathroom cupboards. Declutter your cars and their boots. Declutter your e-mail inbox. Throw away rubbish. Resist the temptation to buy more things with your credit card. When you have finished, ask yourself again (and again), "Is everything in my home and environment as simple as it can be?" Only then can you begin to declutter your mind.

2) Changing your mindset

The Autism mind thinks in absolutes. It is very black and white. Tell this mind that it has had a complete and fresh reinstallation. This new version has an upgraded way of thinking about yourself and others. Click on the print button and pin up a printout of the below to place around your home: Crisis should be viewed as a golden opportunity for transformation. You need to delete the old to create space for the new. Everything that happens in your life, no matter how bad it may seem always has a positive intention. Go with the flow of life change. Do not resist or battle it. You cannot drive forwards if you are constantly looking in the rear-view mirror. Always show compassion towards yourself and others. Release judgement and resentment. Forgive others and yourself. Start with the people living with you. Imagine your thoughts as clouds. Observe them, let them pass and let them go. Avoid interpreting them. Do not compare yourself to others. No one is universally liked.

3) Empower yourself

According to Lao-tzu, an ancient Chinese Philosopher and writer, "Knowing others is intelligence; knowing yourself is true wisdom. Mastering others is strength; mastering yourself is true power." No one changes until you do. You are in control of your own destiny. This is why I developed my own self-help programme. As a person with Autism, you should definitely take charge of yourself. Feeling in control this way will make you feel good.

4) Good sleep for restoration and regeneration

I regarded this as leaving the computer on overnight to download a new programme or perform an update. In the same way, your mind and body need the restorative and regenerative powers of adequate sleep. I tried different amounts and times of sleep. I went to bed earlier and woke up earlier. I went to bed late and woke up later. I tried my daily schedule on regular morning shifts, afternoon shifts, evening shifts and even overnight shifts where I would be awake at night and sleep during the day.

My cat regenerating

The key thing to remember is that everyone has a different sleep or circadian rhythm. Some of us are owls and others are larks. Teenagers function best sleeping late and starting their day late. By researching the sleep patterns of close family members to determine my genetic predisposition, using a 2-week sleep diary and Fitbit watch, I discovered that I functioned best sleeping early and waking up early in the summer months and sleeping late and waking up late in winter. Peak mental performance was usually in the late afternoon and early evenings. I aimed for 10-11 hours of sleep during my recovery period which is more than the recommended 7-8hours for any adult. If you had to choose between consistent sleep and wake times, having a consistent wake up time is probably more important, regardless of when you went to sleep. You should also aim for a sleep efficiency of at least 80%, which means that at least 80% of your time in bed is spent asleep, not tossing and turning.

You may have read much about sleep hygiene and if you are a health professional even educated others about it. You need to practise what you preach and of all the good sleep tips, the ones that worked best for me were decluttering my bedroom and reducing it to the essentials, avoiding exposure to any devices which emit light in the blue spectrum two hours before bed and not sleeping during the day. Avoid watching the evening news, fantasy, action shows and social media which are often full of drama and negativity. You need to steer yourself away from the chaos of electronic life. It also helped me for a while to listen to

Sleep Hypnosis audio tracks which can be heard for free on YouTube. You can choose tracks that run for 8-9 hours. The background noise also helped drown out any anxious ruminations during the night. It was a good sign of recovery when I realised I no longer needed to listen to these tracks to fall asleep and stay asleep each night.

Depending on what medications your doctor has prescribed, the pattern and nature of your dreams may also change. Some medications suppress dreams, others make them more vivid, still others cause nightmares and others cause a rebound of dreams when you stop them. You should talk to your doctor about any distressing and disturbing dreams particularly if they are associated with your medications. I found myself dreaming more and unfortunately experienced quite bad nightmares about my work and losses. When they reached its peak, I recounted my dreams in a daily dream journal which helped. Writing and sketching them brought them out of my head.

5) Stress Management

The body is in a perpetual sympathetic response when stressed. The pupils are larger. The heart rate, breathing and blood pressure are higher and more variable. The stress response has many harmful effects on the body. The best way to enhance the parasympathetic (relaxation) response is by deep breathing to help you focus on the present moment and relax. Focusing on the past increases depression and focusing on the future exacerbates anxiety. The mouth is for eating. The nose is for breathing. The Autism mind is easily distracted and will tend to deviate when you try to do any form of breathing and mindfulness exercises. Therefore, focus on a spot on your body such as your forehead and connect it with your breath. Breathe in for a count of 5, hold for a count of 5 and breathe out for a count of 7. Do this ten times. Meditation itself did not work for me as my concentration frequently wavered. I found it hard to sit still for extended periods of time. I could definitely concentrate better while walking. If you do decide to try it out for yourself, I recommend you start with 10 minutes and then build it up gradually to your limit.

6) **Food, fluids and elimination**

You are what you eat (and drink). The most powerful medicine is in fact the food and water that you consume. In the face of crisis, you are often dehydrated as your body is focussed on doing other things instead of drinking. I initially did not realise that my mouth was dry from medications. I was dizzy and constipated. Hunger was mistaken for thirst. I was drinking hard tap water which did not taste good. I recommend that you drink at least 8 glasses of spring water a day. I set an hourly timer to drink a glass every hour with half a lemon added. The brain fog lifted. My thinking became clearer. The dizziness and constipation disappeared.

Fibre, good quality fats and lean proteins are essential for stabilising your blood sugar levels. Foods should be organic and whole based to help with your recovery. Fruits, vegetables of different colours, nuts (walnuts, almonds, pistachios), seeds (chia, sunflower, pepitas), and fresh lean meats are highly recommended. I appreciated two eggs and an avocado a day. I reminded myself to eat like a Queen at breakfast, a King at lunch and a Pauper at dinner. Working professionals tend to eat like a Pauper at lunch and a King at dinner which is not good for metabolism. I developed a habit of walking to the supermarket two nights a week, an hour before closing time to improve my physical fitness and to look out for any closing specials. It was also much quieter and friendlier for the Autism senses at night. I called these my supermarket surveys and made it a point to concentrate on the outer aisles where the fresh, natural and organically based foods are. Going into a supermarket regardless of the time of the day can still be challenging for a person with Autism. The fresh food aisles are also more open which can increase anxiety. You can feel more exposed. I overcame this by first choosing two aisles that I felt safe in that I could withdraw to whenever I felt too anxious in the open aisles. Another useful technique was starting off in the closed aisles (magazines, electronic equipment) and then the open aisles to beat the anxiety. Doing your own grocery shopping is essential so that you can take ownership of what you eat, in addition to how you eat and who you are being when you eat. On this point, I learnt to eat at more consistent times during the day. Metabolism is best midday to early afternoon. I also used a timer to give myself at least15-20 minutes for each meal. Digestion begins in the mouth.

It is highly likely as a working doctor or busy professional that you are wolfing or gobbling down your lunch. For the sake of your health, slow down and ask yourself, "Who am I being as I am putting this food in my mouth?". Take time to chew your food at least 10 times before swallowing. I drew a picture of my ideal healthy plate and pinned it upon the fridge. Half the plate consisted of lightly cooked vegetables, one quarter clean sourced protein such as wild caught salmon, pasture raised, hormone and antibiotic free chicken, one quarter complex carbohydrates and within this a small portion of healthy fats such as avocado and walnuts. There is often a temptation to snack between meals and reach for the fridge door at night just before bed. Not only is this bad for sleep hygiene but it can also contribute to unnecessary sugar consumption. Remember that it is sugar and not fat that makes you fat. I placed a written reminder on the fridge door, "what am I truly hungry for when I reach for the fridge?"

I finally discovered the reason for the chronic headaches and abdominal pains I had as a child. I had an undiagnosed gluten and dairy sensitivity. This was also having a negative impact on my mood, sleep and anxiety. I highly recommend that you research and trial an elimination of gluten and dairy from your diet. Some of you may need to take it a step further by going egg and soy free. Try it out for a month. You may find as I did that the nose no longer runs after a meal. You may also fall asleep faster, stay asleep more soundly and think more clearly.

Other potential triggers to anxiety are coffee and processed foods. Replace coffee with green tea for its antioxidant effects. Have a handful of almonds and walnuts in a resealable bag for you to snack on when needed. You can carefully swallow a small handful if you are not able to chew them due to your Autism sensitivities. I discovered Acai berries later on during my research and came to appreciate how they can be a great way to start off your day. These berries originate from the Amazon and possess the highest antioxidant content of any berry. You can purchase these berries whole or in powder form and blend them with raspberries, blueberries and strawberries as a smoothie to lighten up your mornings. Finally, for anyone with Autism who likes chocolate, you should go for pure dark chocolate (70-80%). This is not only a healthy form of fat, but it will also boost the feelgood chemicals in your body in a natural way.

7) Sunshine, nature and Vitamin D

I am quite sure that there is a seasonal component to my mood. It is better in spring and summer (before it becomes too hot) and down in winter, especially when the skies are grey. During my darkest days, I went to the beach with my parents when the skies were blue.

We enjoyed having a picnic lunch while soaking in the fresh air and soothing sound of the waves. I recommend 15-30 minutes a day. If you are living in a location where sunshine is scarce, my advice is not to live in darkness, especially if you have any sensory sensitivities towards light and temperature. Wear sunglasses inside the house if you have to but allow some sunlight to come through. The light that enters the back of your eyes helps to entrain your circadian rhythm and improve sleep when it is dark. Open the curtains and let the air and light shine into your room each morning. Turn up the lights during the day in your home and office. Invest in a good quality UV free 10,000 lux phototherapy lamp with a timer which can be set to 30 to 120 minutes each morning. It is likely that persons with Autism have lower Vitamin D levels. We prefer to stay indoors and spend too much time in front of electronic devices watching TV or gaming. Low Vitamin D levels have also been implicated in depression. By exposing yourself to sunlight, you will stimulate your body to produce Vitamin D naturally. You can get your levels checked through a blood test and I recommend you aim for a level of 60-70. If this is difficult to achieve, try Vitamin D capsules from the natural section of your Pharmacy.

I found gardening and walking amongst the trees therapeutic. Gardening is a good isolatory activity when you need to recharge. You can wear gloves if you are concerned about germs. Have a walk through the Garden Centre at night when it is less crowded or during office hours which will also get you some sunshine. I particularly enjoyed looking at the flowers and herbs. Walking among the plants and the trees taught me to appreciate our natural resources better. It is not *nature vs nurture*. It is *nature needs nurture*. I planted parsley, coriander, tomatoes, paw paw, ficus, bonsais and succulents. I experimented with cultivating succulents in an indoor terrarium with artificial lighting which worked well as long as I gave the plants time outdoors as well.

8) Address negative habits

So far, we have talked about the good things to do but there are also bad things that should be avoided. There will be a greater tendency to focus the Autism one-track mind on unhealthy habits which can then become obsessions that spiral out of control. This includes sedentary habits like gaming online, eating junk food, smoking, drinking alcohol, shopping online excessively for gadgets, gambling and even sex. My key advice is to approach any obsessions and addictions with compassion and curiosity. Do not engage in a battle or feel like you are at war with them. Focus instead on the why beneath the why. Which important underlying area of your life are you trying to nourish and overcome? It may be loneliness, stress, boredom, anxiety and depression. Focus your energies on addressing these and you will find the negative habits disappearing on their own spontaneously.

9) Physical movement

As a working person with Autism, I was focussed like a laser beam on two desktop computer screens, a smartphone, iPad, a smart watch and TV screen in each room. These screens are like a tornado vortex that continually sucks you in. The poor posture that I had led to headaches, neck crepitus (creaking and cracking), a stiff shoulder and painful sleep. A correct posture is essential for neurological functioning and there is not much point in seeing a Physiotherapist, Remedial Masseur and Chiropractor if you do not make the personal effort to address the underlying screen issues and need for regular physical movement away from the devices. I realised that to change the emotion, I needed to change the motion. I invested in a fitness watch (these can range from tens to hundreds of dollars) which was very useful in tracking my movement and sleep. Some watches send you a weekly update with a graph and how your steps, heart rate and sleep went. I recommend that you aim for 5,000 steps a day initially and build it up to 10,000 steps a day. A movement break after every 15 minutes of sitting still is essential. You can programme the fitness watch to give you a vibratory reminder.

Coordination and clumsiness are often issues for those on the Autism spectrum. I did not find joining a gym and any intense workouts appealing. Slower forms of exercise are much better by simply adding spring to my step while walking and swinging my arms actively. You are more likely to be motivated to walk if there is a purpose and destination. For me, it was walking to the video kiosk, window shopping and visiting the fresh food aisles after business hours when it was less busy. The use of vibration platforms is controversial, especially when weight loss is the aim. However, I found it tremendously useful and relaxing as it stimulated movement in my legs and overall body. I could do this indoors while listening to music or an audiobook. Some of you may find running on a treadmill too strenuous. I discovered that it was not good for my mind as running on the spot exacerbated obsessive thinking. To overcome my screen addiction,

I printed out a notice for myself on the fridge and next to each screen which read:

Mind and Body Scan
Unplug and put away devices
Consider others
Walk outside or jump on platform

I shall now speak about Qi Gong which is a traditional Chinese centring and mindfulness practice for health and healing. Qi is regarded as the life force energy in nature and the whole universe. It also means breath, air and vitality. It is the force that animates the body and brings it to life. Qi needs to flow to treat and prevent depression and anxiety. In the study of Qi Gong, there are 5 nature elements that form the basic principles for moving the body. Relaxation (water element), resiliency (wood element), enjoyment (fire element), centring (earth element) and energy (metal element). You will also learn about the six healing sounds (Sssss, Chwoooo, Shhhhh, Haww, Whooo and Heeee). While it will be useful to have the support of a Qi Gong teacher, I taught myself using a self-help book (see reference section), Qi healing cards and YouTube video exercises for anxiety, depression and trauma release which can be done at home for free.

10) An attitude of gratefulness whatever the circumstances

When you are experiencing a sudden life change, a crisis, an illness or a loss, it is easy for the mind with Autism to hyperfocus on the negative. This includes what you have lost and rehearsing in your mind repeatedly what you could have done to prevent the loss. Instead, you should start each day and end each day considering what you still have and are grateful for. There is always someone else less fortunate than you. Do not waste your energy comparing yourself with someone whom you think is in a better position. Money does not buy long lasting happiness.

11) Hobbies to boost creativity and self-expression

The mind with Autism needs to have a mission and a purpose. It needs to be continually stimulated and nourished with positive activities. For me, it was a mindfulness colouring book, gardening, listening to classical music and repairing Lego®. This is a time in which you can rekindle childhood hobbies and Lego® is one that can appeal to the mind with Autism. It is structured and predictable. There is a tangible outcome. It is visually appealing. There are clear instructions to follow. You can do this alone or with a friend. Specific Lego® themes that appealed to me during my recovery were Architecture®, Star Wars® and Technic®. Reading was a childhood hobby, but I found it very difficult to concentrate. Try audiobook versions of your favourites which can be easily found online. I could concentrate much better while listening and moving at the same time.

12) Animals

An adoring cat

Many people on the Autism spectrum relate better to animals than humans. I am not quite sure why, but I always felt immediately at ease with cats. Others on the spectrum may have a phobia of certain animals such as dogs. Find a favourite animal (which could even be fish) and take the time to care for them. If you are living in a small space, setting up an aquarium should be considered. You may wish to avoid rearing fish with any territorial or aggressive tendencies such as Cichlids or Siamese fighting fish which can be countertherapeutic. Animals are non-judgemental.

They accept you for who you are and perhaps that is the most important thing for a person on the Autism spectrum.

13) Connect with and volunteer to help others

I found this very difficult to do and would understand this for anyone on the Autism spectrum. The tendency is to withdraw into yourself and perhaps hope for someone to reach out to you. I can tell you that you are likely to have to wait for a very long time for this to happen if you leave it to others. Getting reconnected is key to recovery. I asked a friend, uncle or aunt to send me a daily quote or message of encouragement. I reached out to people whom I knew and asked them to connect with me over the phone, via video link or in person from time to time. It is during times of difficulty that you will discover who your true friends really are. Some people whom I thought were close to me disappeared and others whom I never imagined would show compassion did. It is important that you connect with likeminded individuals who share a joint interest. Ask yourself how you feel following your interactions with them to gauge how nourishing it was for your Autism mind. If you are finding it difficult to connect with those at home, use nonverbal means of communication such as notes, texts and emails. This is better than no communication. Setting aside a prescribed time each week to meet face to face to "talk about issues" is likely to be too confronting.

You should devote a day a week in which you can be of service to others. This may include phoning someone whom you know is going through a difficult period, sorting out and giving away possessions that you no longer need, volunteering at an animal shelter and cooking for charity. Use your online research instincts to find ways in which you can be of service to others. If you are able, donate 10% of the money you earn. This will nourish your altruistic nature which is a strength of Autism.

14) Connect to something greater

The scientific mind with Autism may not believe that there is such a thing as God but the connection with that which is greater looks and feels different for each individual person. For me, this meant surrendering or releasing what I could not control, drawing strength from a deeper connection with myself, making choices and taking action in areas where I could. I was brought up in a traditional Catholic environment where prayers and various rituals were part of religious practice. I have a tendency for obsessive thinking and even compulsive praying where I would need to pray a certain number of times until it felt just right or some harm would come over me or my family. While this may have been an important means of connection for me in the past, you need to ask yourself in what ways can this connection still work for you now? Connection can also occur through deep breathing, Qi Gong, helping others and anything else that may leave you feeling nourished and at peace with yourself.

15) Set yourself free from a dependency on medications

I feel it is important to have a solid foundation of positive lifestyle habits when considering the number and types of medications that you really need to be on. Side effects are always a concern with medications that work on your mind. You never really know what the long-term effects are. While they may be useful in the acute period, you need to ask yourself whether you still really need it in the long term. It is very important that you discuss this with your doctor as it varies from person to person.

16) Visual schedule for the week

When you have a better idea of what your week should look like, type this into a weekly schedule so that you can see for yourself how balanced it is. Are there any areas that still seem excessive or obsessive? Do you have enough physical activity? How often are you connecting with others? Persons with Autism are creatures of routine and habit. Unfortunately, the only constant thing in this universe is change. Allow yourself three flexible moments in your weekly schedule in which you know that you can add or delete three activities if things did not go according to plan.

17) Connection with a Coach and Mentor

Accountability is the key to achieving your goals. It is particularly important in Autism to have someone that you can report to. I highly recommend that you find yourself an Autism Coach who has been trained in the art of coaching and habit change to hold you accountable to whatever goals you set for yourself to change your lifestyle habits. This is not the same as seeing a Doctor, Psychologist, Counsellor or Therapist. A Coach does not diagnose or treat. This distinction is particularly important. The best way forward is to find yourself a Coach to work in partnership with your doctors. Any actions that your doctors wish implemented can also be supported by your Coach. As for me, I realised that what I needed was someone who could also support me with the fundamental lifestyle issues who was cost effective and flexible. I needed someone who was willing to come out to me as it was stressful facing traffic and finding parking. Sitting in the waiting room also exacerbated anxiety especially when the doctor was running late. I also needed someone who was willing to connect with me over the phone or via video link. Surprisingly, I found coaching and mentoring over the phone very effective as there was no pressure for me to analyse the nonverbal cues of the person I was speaking to. I could just concentrate on the voice, report back on what I had accomplished for the week, speak about any challenges or obstacles I had in achieving those goals and a clear step forward before the next phone session. My Coach had also experienced failure in life and could relate to what I was going through. I gained practical ideas from him and he helped me put my circumstances into a better perspective. Listening to his own story was also deeply inspirational.

Here are important red flags for you as a doctor with Autism that should indicate the need to reach out for assistance:

- Feelings of emptiness and loneliness despite being successful at work
- Trouble falling asleep, staying asleep and early morning awakening
- Eating beyond satisfaction in the evenings and missing out on lunches
- Racing thoughts especially at night
- Feeling like you are working too hard and achieving little
- Increased obsessional thinking and irritability towards others especially your family and staff
- Using alcohol, caffeine, over the counter pills and any substances to regulate your mood and sleep
- Lifestyle creep with the urge to spend whatever you earn particularly online

- Turning down any invitations from family or friends to do anything outside of work
- A tight feeling in the chest especially after work
- Getting more disorganised and absent minded at work
- Increased in sensory sensitivities such as sound, touch and temperature

Here are some tips on how you can be a better patient:

Be patient in finding a doctor who is Autism friendly. Arrange an extended consultation. Survey the area online to determine its location, parking and nature of surrounding businesses. Ring ahead to find out how your doctor is running for time and only enter the practice five minutes before you can be seen. Prepare a one-page summary before your first appointment to give to your doctor explaining your Autism strengths, weaknesses, what you prefer to communicate verbally and what you prefer to communicate in writing. Tell your doctor if you feel uncomfortable with eye contact. Make sure that you each have a turn at speaking. Have a list of items to discuss during your appointment. Do not sit directly face to face with your doctor as this will be too confronting and exhausting without you realising it. Insist that you and your doctor sit at a 45-degree angle to each other. It is OK to bring a trusted person with you to the appointment who can also remind you if anything further needs to be discussed.

In summary, through my recovery, I am now ready to embark on a new life phase building on the lessons that I have learnt. I am determined to continue to lead a simple and decluttered life, not possess anything that I do not require and set up whatever I have using the principles of Feng Shui. This adopts basic energy principles in determining the placement of objects so that they are in harmony with your environment. To me, it provides a common-sense approach to how a simple and decluttered environment can be achieved to help you feel good. I can also use the principles of Eastern Philosophy to create a spiritual balance in my life. This includes a mindfulness approach focussing on the present moment. Accept the things that I cannot change, have the courage to change the things that I can and the wisdom to know the difference.

Chapter Eight
The Gift of Autism

For far too long now, Autism has been viewed as a disorder, condition or disability. Indeed, under the Diagnostic and Statistical Manual 5th Edition of the American Psychiatric Association, Autism Spectrum **Disorder** is diagnosed when the following criteria are met:

A. Persistent deficits in social communication and social interaction across multiple contexts, as manifested by the following, currently or by history:

1. **Deficits** in social-emotional reciprocity, ranging, for example, from **abnormal** social approach and **failure** of normal back-and-forth conversation; to reduced sharing of interests, emotions, or affect; to **failure** to initiate or respond to social interactions.
2. **Deficits** in nonverbal communicative behaviours used for social interaction, ranging, for example, from **poorly** integrated verbal and nonverbal

communication; to **abnormalities** in eye contact and body language or **deficits** in understanding and use of gestures; to a **total lack** of facial expressions and nonverbal communication.

3. **Deficits** in developing, maintaining, and understanding relationships, ranging, for example, from **difficulties** adjusting behaviour to suit various social contexts; to **difficulties** in sharing imaginative play or in making friends; to absence of interest in peers.

B. Restricted, repetitive patterns of behaviour, interests, or activities, as manifested by at least two of the following, currently or by history:

1. Stereotyped or repetitive motor movements, use of objects, or speech (e.g., simple motor stereotypies, lining up toys or flipping objects, echolalia, idiosyncratic phrases). 2. Insistence on sameness, inflexible adherence to routines, or ritualised patterns or verbal nonverbal behaviour (e.g., **extreme** distress at small changes, **difficulties** with transitions, **rigid** thinking patterns, greeting rituals, need to take the same route or eat food every day).

3. **Highly** restricted, fixated interests that are abnormal in intensity or focus (e.g., strong attachment to or preoccupation with unusual objects, **excessively** circumscribed or perseverative interests).

4. **Hyper-** or **hypo**reactivity to sensory input or unusual interest in sensory aspects of the environment (e.g., apparent indifference to pain/temperature, **adverse** response to specific sounds or textures, **excessive** smelling or touching of objects, visual fascination with lights or movement).

C. Symptoms must be present in the early developmental period (but may not become fully manifest until social demands exceed limited capacities, or may be masked by learned strategies in later life).

D. Symptoms cause clinically significant **impairment** in social, occupational, or other important areas of current functioning.

E. These **disturbances** are not better explained by Intellectual **Disability** (Intellectual Developmental **Disorder**) or Global Developmental **Delay**.

Intellectual **Disability** and Autism Spectrum **Disorder** frequently co-occur; to make comorbid diagnoses of Autism Spectrum **Disorder** and Intellectual **Disability**, social communication should be below that expected for general developmental level.

Specify if: with or without accompanying intellectual **impairment**; associated with a known medical or genetic condition or environmental factor (Coding note: Use additional code to identify the associated medical or genetic condition.); associated with another neurodevelopmental, mental, or behavioural **disorder** (Coding note: Use additional code[s] to identify the associated neurodevelopmental, mental, or behavioural **disorder**[s].); with catatonia (refer to the criteria for catatonia associated with another **mental disorder**, pp. 119-120, for definition) (Coding note: Use additional code 293.89 [F06.1]; catatonia associated with Autism Spectrum **Disorder** to indicate the presence of the comorbid catatonia.)

Specify current **severity**: Severity is based on social communication impairments and restricted, repetitive patterns of behaviour.

Level 3 "Requiring very substantial support": **Severe deficits** in verbal and nonverbal social communication skills cause **severe impairments** in functioning, **very limited** initiation of social interactions, and **minimal response** to social overtures from others. For example, a person with inflexibility of behaviour, **extreme difficulty** coping with change, or other restricted/repetitive behaviours that markedly interfere with functioning in all spheres.

Level 2 "Requiring substantial support": **Marked deficits** in verbal and nonverbal social communication skills; social **impairments** apparent even with supports in place; **limited** initiation of social interactions; and **reduced** or **abnormal** responses to social overtures from others. For example, a person who speaks simple sentences, whose interaction is limited to narrow special interests, and who has markedly odd nonverbal communication, inflexibility of behaviour, difficulty coping with change, or other restricted/repetitive behaviours that appear frequently enough to be obvious to the casual observer and interfere with functioning in a variety of contexts.

Level 1 "Requiring support": Without supports in place, **deficits** in social communication cause **noticeable impairments**. Difficulty initiating social interactions, and clear examples of **atypical or unsuccessful** response to social overtures of others. May appear to have decreased interest in social interactions. For example, a person who is able to speak in full sentences and engages in communication but in whom to- and-fro conversation with others **fails**, and whose **inflexibility** of behaviour causes significant **interference** with functioning in one or more contexts. **Difficulty** switching between activities. **Problems** of organization and planning **hamper** independence. Attempts to make friends are **odd** and **typically unsuccessful**.

While these criteria can be helpful for professionals to communicate their findings and obtain resources, support and even funding for the person concerned, there are inherent risks associated with diagnostic labels, particularly for the person who is recognised as having Autism. Within the diagnostic criteria, I have highlighted the terms used such as "deficits, failure, abnormal, poorly, difficulties, extreme, excessive, problems, unsuccessful and impairment", all of which are highly judgmental terms that can destroy the self-esteem of children, adults and their parents. These criteria are readily available online. It is extremely easy for the mind with Autism to zoom in on the negative terms used.

To some individuals, it may seem incredulous that such terms and criteria can be used without an objective blood test, brain scan or a gold standard to verify the diagnosis. Rather, a lifelong disorder is diagnosed based on descriptions and subjective opinion of the person(s) who completes the assessment on an individual whose presentation can vary from day to day and indeed can improve over time.

I was diagnosed as a doctor with Autism Spectrum Disorder Level 1. Although the diagnosis provided a sense of relief and explained many of the challenges I experienced, I was concerned that it would become an excuse to not undertake social activities, to avoid crowds, not make friends and not look at others in the eye as per the diagnostic criteria. I could not do anything for myself because I was a failure, abnormal and impaired. DO NOT let this be the case for you.

It has been noted in various parts of the literature that suitable jobs for those on the Autism Spectrum include:
- Graphic Designer
- Computer Programmer
- Computer technician or operator
- Research Scientist
- Medical Research Scientist
- Architect
- Pharmacist
- Animal Scientist and Conservationist
- Library Science
- Commercial Art
- Drafting
- Copy Editing
- I would add to this list Car Detailer

The unsuitable jobs are:
- Salesman
- Manager
- Solicitor or Lawyer
- Police Officer
- Doctor, Dentist or Health Inspector

- Secondary School Teacher
- Airline Pilot
- Waitress
- Cashier
- Short order Cook
- Casino Dealer
- Airline ticket Agent
- Air traffic Controller
- Receptionist
- Telephone operator

If I had come across this list in high school and knew that I was on the spectrum, it is highly possible that I would not have entered university to study Medicine. With the benefit of hindsight, I think it is timely for this list to be updated as there are many jobs, previously deemed unsuitable that could work for a person on the spectrum. It is not just IT, Accountancy, the world of Academia and even Engineering. I would argue that medical doctors on the Autism Spectrum are an expanding frontier.

Therefore, it is my firm belief that the signs and symptoms of Autism need to be reframed and the words disability and disorder removed from the mindset of anyone with Autism and those who support them. To the best of my ability, I avoided using these terms in my medical reports and always prefaced them with the strengths of the individual concerned.

Based on my personal and professional experience, there are many traits of Autism that are highly desirable for success in life. Many of my university colleagues and teachers possessed Autism characteristics. They were unique individuals, highly altruistic and placed great emphasis on service to others.

There are solid reasons why one can enter a career in Medicine and work as a Social Scientist, as I did in Psychiatry or a Natural Scientist such as Radiology or Pathology or both as a Research Scientist in any discipline. In other words, being on the Autism Spectrum is not a contraindication to becoming a doctor.

Doctors with Autism can be also be good managers, provided that you are able to resist the temptation of focusing on the details and micromanaging others as leading people will be the most challenging aspect. One has to be able to keep a distance, make a right and not necessarily the most popular decision. Doctors can also be good Entrepreneurs, particularly as an entrepreneur of creative ideas.

I now realise that Autism is a gift that continues to enable me to survive and thrive. I refer to the Discovery criteria for Aspie by Tony Attwood and Carol Gray (with some additions, I have placed a ✔ next to the ones that apply to me and a ✔✔✔ to the ones that particularly apply):

A. A qualitative advantage in social interaction, as manifested by a majority of the following:

- peer relationships characterised by absolute loyalty and impeccable dependability ✔
- free of sexist, "age-ist", or cultural biases; ability to regard others at "face value" ✔
- speaking one's mind irrespective of social context or adherence to personal beliefs ✔
- ability to pursue personal theory or perspective despite conflicting evidence ✔
- seeking an audience or friends capable of enthusiasm for unique interests and topics, consideration of details, spending time

discussing a topic that may not be of primary interest to others ✔

- listening without continual judgement or assumption ✔ ✔ ✔
- interested primarily in significant contributions to conversation; preferring to avoid "ritualistic small talk" or socially trivial statements and superficial conversation ✔
- seeking sincere, positive, genuine friends with an unassuming sense of humour ✔ ✔ ✔

B. Fluent in "Aspergerese", a social language characterised by at least three of the following:

- a **determination** to seek the truth ✔
- conversation free of hidden meaning or agenda ✔
- **advanced** vocabulary and interest in words ✔
- fascination with word-based humour, such as puns ✔
- advanced use of metaphor ✔

C. Cognitive skills characterised by at least four of the following:

- **strong** preference for detail over gestalt (but also strong ability to see the gestalt) ✔
- original, often unique perspective in problem solving ✔ ✔ ✔
- **exceptional** memory and/or recall of details often forgotten or disregarded by others, for example: names, dates, schedules, routines ✔ ✔ ✔
- **avid** perseverance in gathering and cataloguing information on a topic of interest ✔ ✔ ✔
- **persistence** of thought ✔ ✔ ✔
- encyclopaedic or "CD rom" knowledge of one or more topics ✔ ✔ ✔
- **knowledge** of routines and a focussed desire to maintain order and accuracy ✔ ✔ ✔
- **clarity** of values/decision making unaltered by political or financial factors ✔

D. Additional possible features:

- acute sensitivity to specific sensory experiences and stimuli, for example: hearing, touch, vision and/or smell ✔
- **strength** in individual sports and games, particularly those involving endurance or visual accuracy, including rowing, swimming, bowling, badminton, tennis, table tennis, chess ✔
- "social unsung hero" with trusting optimism: frequent victim of social weaknesses of others, while **steadfast** in the belief of the possibility of genuine friendship ✔
- increased probability over general population of attending university after high school ✔
- often take care of others outside the range of typical development ✔ ✔ ✔

A Tutor of the Year in Medical School advised that Medicine is different from other professions because we are not dealing with buildings, worn down teeth, the intricacies of the law, nor the construction of roads; we are dealing with people. I affirm that it is entirely possible for a person on the Autism spectrum, despite the social diversity or difference to be able to learn the skills to deal with people. Although it may not come naturally, just as it was for me, I was able to learn and train myself to practice Medicine with humility, compassion, dedication, honesty, predictability and altruism. In the field of Psychiatry, I was able to play the part of an emotion's detective. I could immerse myself in areas to build my sense of self-worth. Without this Psychiatric journey, I would not have discovered my true sense of self. I would not have had the opportunity to use losses and challenges to map out a better direction in my career and life.

As I have pointed out, these Discovery Criteria are also the essential characteristics of an outstanding doctor. Medicine itself is a diverse spectrum of opportunities. You can choose a subspecialty based on your social/emotional and personal interest profile. There are no particular stereotypes and the examples below are purely based on personal experience.

If you have a preference for the natural sciences, you may wish to consider:

- Anaesthesia

- Clinical Pharmacology
- Dermatology
- Gastroenterology and Hepatology
- Immunology and Allergy
- Infectious Diseases
- Oncology
- Ophthalmology
- Pathology
- Respiratory and Sleep Medicine
- Sexual Health Medicine

If you have an inclination towards social sciences in addition to natural sciences:

- Addiction Medicine
- Endocrinology
- General Medicine
- Geriatric Medicine
- Neurology
- Nephrology
- Occupational and Environmental Medicine
- Pain Medicine
- Palliative Medicine

- Psychiatry
- Rehabilitation Medicine
- Rheumatology

If you particularly enjoy seeing and talking with people:
- General Practice
- Paediatrics and Child Health (dealing with parents!)
- Psychiatry

If you are predisposed to a black and white style of thinking:
- Cardiology
- Clinical Genetics
- Gastroenterology and Hepatology
- Oncology
- Sports and Exercise Medicine
- Surgery

If you prefer to spend less time talking with patients:
- Haematology
- Intensive Care Medicine (more time talking with staff and families)

- Medical Administration
- Nuclear Medicine
- Pathology, including Forensic Pathology
- Public Health Medicine
- Research of any kind
- Surgery
- Radiology

If you like being a Manager and/or have entrepreneurial skills:
- Medical Administration

The subspecialties that may be more challenging due to the unpredictable nature of the work and challenging systems:

- Child and Adolescent Psychiatry
- Emergency Medicine
- Medical Oncology
- Obstetrics and Gynaecology
- Paediatrics and Child Health
- Palliative Care

It should also be noted that there are certain specialties where self-care is particularly important, as they are associated with higher rates of burnout and suicide. These specialties which have been noted in the list above include Psychiatry, Anaesthesia and General Practice.

The speciality that you choose should also focus on your strengths. The ones that come naturally to a person with Autism include positive personality traits such as dedication, commitment, perseverance, intelligence, creativity, loyalty, tangible skills such as logical thinking, memory and talents such as researching and analysing. The knowledge and the skills that you have are super valuable resources.

More importantly, you should discover early on your limitations in Medicine. Unfortunately, I had to learn this the hard way. A career in Developmental Paediatrics and Child Health as well as Child and Adolescent Psychiatry is not recommended unless:

- you know and accept that you have Autism yourself
- you acknowledge that there are inherent risks in seeing individuals who have far too much in common with you

- you are acutely aware of the dangers of losing insight about your own health
- you accept the importance of formal support and have them in place to care for your social and emotional wellbeing
- you take responsibility for your own actions
- you avoid sitting and waiting for someone
- you know when to call for help
- you know when the traits such as intense focus can be a strength, when they are a weakness and be able to use them strategically.

In short, any career in Medicine in possible with the right support, understanding and assistance. This includes support to negotiate the social world around you and to put things in perspective. It is highly encouraged that you have a Coach or Mentor work alongside you in your capacity as a medical student or doctor. This is not just a generic Coach or Mentor but a person who has special expertise in mentoring or coaching individuals on the Autism Spectrum and who has had a share of the experiences that you are going through. The Coach or Mentor can be a doctor who has "come out" as being on the spectrum who is willing to connect with you regularly, at least once a week to talk about successes, challenges and provide assistance and accountability from the perspective of a wise fellow with Autism.

Conclusion and Dedication

Thank you for taking the time to read this book. I hope that regardless of your background, you have found this a helpful resource. Above all else, please know that you have a right to be accepted and to be happy for who you are.

I would like to make special mention of my parents who have been there for me always, through the thick and thin, the ups and downs. Thank you also to all my family, especially my dear sister, grandmother, uncles, aunties and my godfather. To all my friends from Medical School, Doctors, Teachers, Supervisors, medical and non-medical colleagues, I am extremely grateful for your time and patience. To those of you who came to my aide when I was at the lowest point of my life, I thank you from the bottom of my heart. A special note to my dear friend from afar, William. Thank you to that which is greater than me from above.

Most importantly, I would like to dedicate this book to all my patients and their families. You have taught me so much about being a neurodiverse person. Thank you for giving me a life purpose and for helping me stay young at heart.

Remember to take charge of your choices and your life. Do not let anyone else do so. The Autism is not you but rather you are your Autism.

References

ABC. (2019). Love on the Spectrum [Video]. Retrieved from https://iview.abc.net.au/show/love-on-the-spectrum

American Psychiatric Association. (2013). *Diagnostic and Statistical Manual of Mental Disorders* (5th Edition). Arlington, VA: Author.

Attwood T. The complete guide to Asperger's syndrome. Jessica Kingsley Publishers; 2006 Sep 28.

Attwood T, Evans C, Lesko A, editors. An Aspie's Guide to Bullying: Been There. Done That. Try This!. Jessica Kingsley Publishers; 2014 Nov 28.

Attwood, T., & Garnett, M. (2016). *Exploring Depression, and Beating the Blues: A CBT Self-Help Guide to Understanding and Coping with Depression in Asperger's Syndrome [ASD-Level 1]*. Jessica Kingsley Publishers.

Bissonnette, B. (2013). *Asperger's Syndrome Workplace Survival Guide: A Neurotypical's Secrets for Success*. Jessica Kingsley Publishers.

Chia, M., & Holden, L. (2011). *Simple Chi Kung: Exercises for Awakening the Life-force Energy*. Simon and Schuster.

Denenburg, D., Isaacs, P., Kupferstein, H., Hane, R. E. J., Krejcha, K., Grandin, T., ... & Willey, L. H. (2014). *Been There. Done That. Try This!: An Aspie's Guide to Life on Earth*. Jessica Kingsley Publishers.

Dickerson, A.S., Pearson, D.A., Loveland K.A., Rahbar M.H. and Filipek, P. A. (2014) Role of parental occupation in autism spectrum disorder diagnosis and severity. *Research in Autism Spectrum Disorders 8* 997-1007.

Felder MA. Asperger Syndrome: Assessing and treating High-Functioning Autism Spectrum Disorders. Guilford Publications; 2014 Apr 1.

Grandin, T. (1999). Choosing the right job for people with Autism or Asperger's syndrome. *Indiana Resources Centre for Autism.*

Hawton, K., Clements, A., Sakarovitch, C., Simkin, S., & Deeks, J. J. (2001). Suicide in doctors: a study of risk according to gender, seniority and specialty in medical practitioners in England and Wales, 1979–

1995. *Journal of Epidemiology & Community Health, 55*(5), 296-300.

Kivunja, C., & Kuyini, A. B. (2017). Understanding and applying research paradigms in educational contexts. *International Journal of Higher Education, 6*(5), 26-41.

Niebuhr, R. (1943). The serenity prayer. *Bulletin of the Federal Council of Churches.*

Salkin, W. (2016, October 14). Loneliness as epidemic [Web log post]. Retrieved from https://blog.petrieflom.law.harvard.edu/2016/10/14/loneliness-as-epidemic/

Whiteman, H. (2017). Loneliness a bigger killer than obesity, say researchers. Retrieved from https://www.medicalnewstoday.com/articles/318723.php#1

Further reading (includes the perspective of employers and colleagues)

https://www.amaze.org.au/wp-content/uploads/2019/06/Amaze-Information-Sheet-Working-with-a-Person-with-Aspergers-Syndrome-Aug-11.pdf

https://www.arghighland.co.uk/pdf/ARGH%20Employment%20leaflet.pdf

https://www.autism.org.uk/professionals/employers/information-for-employers.aspx

https://network.autism.org.uk/search/node/employment

https://www.jobaccess.gov.au/employers/employer-toolkit

http://www.onethingforautism.com.au/

http://specialisterne.com/

https://www.tuc.org.uk/research-analysis/reports/autism-workplace

Adulthood, Program 3. (2018). https://www.autismcrc.com.au/our-programs/adulthood

Grossberg, B. (2015). *Asperger's and Adulthood. A Guide to Working, Loving, and Living with Asperger's Syndrome.* Althea Press, Berkeley, California.

Noordsy, D. L. (Ed.). (2019). *Lifestyle Psychiatry.* American Psychiatric Pub.

Schneider, M & Bogden, J. (2017). *An Employer's Guide to Managing Professionals on the Autism Spectrum.* Jessica Kingsley Publishers, London and Philadelphia.

Stanford, A. (2011). *Business for Aspies: 42 Best Practices for Using Asperger Syndrome Traits at Work Successfully.* Jessica Kingsley Publishers, London and Philadelphia.

INDEX

A

Academic 36, 51, 109

Acceptance
  of self 35, 40, 46, 165-166

Accountability 131, 168, 197, 223

Advocacy 129

Anaesthesia 86, 217, 221

Anchors 92

Animals, also see pets 30-31, 46, 61, 108, 137, 192-193

Anxiety 3, 40-41, 54, 57, 88-89, 94, 117, 134, 144, 151, 158-159, 168, 186, 198
  exercises 178, 190
  depression 100, 156
  prevention 45
  social 59-60
  stress 94, 113, 144, 147, 160, 178, 186
  treatment 111, 129
  triggers 182

B

Bedside manner 82

Behavioural Sciences, Public Health and General Practice 72-73

Beliefs 14, 104, 122-125

Blind 87, 162-163

Bullying 38
  childhood 50
  workplace 99, 129

Burnout 149, 221

Business
  meetings 130
  setting up 133-134, 149

C

Camouflage, also see faking it 6, 163

Caring for yourself, see self-care

Cats 192-193

Change 1, 104, 114, 121, 130, 150, 165-166, 170, 187, 202
- attitude 147
- coping with 120, 207
- lifestyle 197
- sudden 155, 190

Church 13, 18, 49, 56
Circadian rhythm 112, 175, 184
Cleaning 95, 136
- cars 21, 57, 63
- compulsive 32, 138
- rituals 155

Clinical Ethics 81
Clinical Microbiology and Laboratory Medicine 76-77
Clinical Pharmacology 85
Clutter, see also decluttering 149
Coach 60, 110, 116, 149, 197-198, 222
Coeducational 28, 34, 36, 40, 57
Cognitive assessment 92

Cognitive Behaviour Therapy (CBT) 111, 129
Colleagues 96-97, 116, 121, 154, 163, 165-166, 226-227
- medical 118
- university 74, 80, 212
- work 107-108

Communication 1, 99, 105, 109, 115-116, 203-204, 207-208
- cards 152
- non verbal 1, 30, 120, 194
- skills 128-129
- styles 121
- verbal 120

Compassion 2, 7, 35, 121, 150, 164, 173, 186, 193, 217
Competition 71, 107
Consultant 105, 129-130
Control 7, 41, 93, 113, 150, 169, 174, 195
- loss of 50, 122, 155, 159, 186

Coordinated Neurosciences 76

Copying, also see mimicry 29, 34, 36, 40, 75, 97, 115
Counselling 60
Crisis 132
   intervention 128, 160, 168, 173, 179, 190
Culture
   eastern 40
Curriculum Vitae (CV) 109

D

Dairy 46, 182
Dating 52, 59
Decluttering 171-172, 176
Depression 53, 55, 57, 71, 159-162, 178, 184, 186
   anxiety 3, 5, 100, 156
   prevention 189
   suicide 45
   treatment 129
Diagnosis 23, 42, 98, 144, 163, 209
   disclosing 89, 109
   self 168
Diet 25, 46, 148, 182

Diplomacy 93, 149
Disclosure 42, 89-91
   sexual identity 60
   workplace 109-110
Discrimination 123
Diversity 96, 110
   medical profession 96
   neurodiversity 96-97, 102, 109-110, 116
   social 217
Dogs 30, 136, 192

E

Empathy 2, 121, 126
Employment 5-6, 110
Engineer 2, 159
Envy 107
Epistemology 124-126
Executive functioning 92
Examinations 81
   clinical 111, 130
   extra time 89
   preparing for 89
Exercise 24, 115, 188
   exposure 111

   meditative 153
   mindfulness 178
Expectations 40, 42, 59, 120, 150
Eye contact 12, 16, 58, 89, 201

F

Faking it, also see camouflage 97, 130
Family 43, 112, 115, 123, 132, 137, 144, 167, 199
   fantasy 116
   history 45, 169
   support 79
   therapy 103, 129
Feelings 13, 44, 150, 164, 168-169, 199
Finances, management of 116
Friendships 1, 44, 47-48, 50, 57-58
Food 61, 69, 179-182
   chewing 181
   junk 186
   organic 179-180
   processed 182

G

General Practice 72-73, 79, 219, 221
General Surgery 86-86
Gluten 46
   elimination 182
   free 148
   sensitivity 22

H

Happy 26, 224
Headaches 22-24, 94, 182, 187
Health 58, 61, 112, 148, 181, 189
   care professionals 159
   chronic 101
   mental 45, 97, 102, 149-15
Help
   asking for 113, 222
   others 8, 22, 101, 149, 193-194
   self 163, 171, 174, 190
High School 51, 54
   transition 145
Hobbies 191

Home
> environment 172
> lights 184
> sharing 169
> visits 72

Homework 17, 29, 33

Human Anatomy 75

Humour 78, 108, 114
> coping mechanism 74, 127, 130

I

Imagination 27, 34, 50, 142

Independence 167, 169

Infectious Diseases 84-85, 218

Insomnia, see sleep

Interests 48, 51, 151
> special 27, 44, 58, 68, 71, 92, 98, 116

Intern 98-100

Isolation 13, 26, 43, 55, 58, 160, 166

J

Job interview 98

Jobs 110
> suitable/recommended 210
> unsuitable 210-211

Job share 113-114

Judgemental 93

L

Labelling, Labels 4, 42, 132, 208

Leadership 109, 121
> clinical 118
> operational 118

Learning 71, 88-92
> alternative 94
> rote 72-74, 78, 111

Lego® 191
> adult fan 134
> developmental stage 137
> expert 142
> golden age 139
> zone 136

LGBTQIAPK (Lesbian, Gay, Bisexual, Transgender, Queer or Querying, Intersex, Asexual, Pansexual, Kink) 54, 60

Lifestyle 112, 115, 133, 171
   creep 157, 197
   habits 186, 196-197
Loneliness 13, 57-58, 71, 186, 199
   and isolation difference 55-56

M
Manager 119, 210, 212, 220
Mask 75, 97
Medical Biomorphology 73
Medical Chemistry 72
Medical Pharmacology 77-78
Medical School 62, 65-68, 89-90
Medicating 132
Medications 148
   dependency 196
   long term effects 132
   self-prescribing 168
   side effects 167-168, 177, 196
Meditation 178
Medicine, Chinese 23

Memory
   eidetic 76
   short term 165
   visual 11, 74, 78
Mental health 45, 97, 102, 149-150
Mental illness, invisible 144, 162
Methods, methodology 125-126
Mentor(s) 60, 110, 113, 142, 149, 197-198, 222
Mimicry, also see copying 36, 40, 43, 48, 75, 97, 111
Mind blindness 87
Mindset 122-123, 212
   changing 114, 173
   victim 165
Mood 158, 182-183, 199
Music 6, 25-26, 55, 68, 188, 191

N
Nature 183-185, 189
   Altruistic 194, 212

Negotiation 93
Neurodivergent 96
Neurodiverse, neurodiversity 5, 96, 99, 102, 109-110, 113, 116
   knowledge 94
   spectrum 96-97
Neuropsychological assessment 92
Neurotypical 5, 18, 41, 43, 59

O

Observation, also see copying, mimicry 18, 23, 43, 48, 111, 126
Obsessions 18, 27, 116, 171-172, 186
Obsessive Compulsive, Obsessive Compulsive Disorder (OCD) 88, 138, 155, 167
Obstetrics and Gynaecology 84, 220
Office politics 106-108
On call 84, 106, 113

Ontology 123-126
Organising 118-120
Ophthalmology 87-88, 218
Otorhinolaryngology 87

P

Paediatrics 83-84, 219-221
Paradigm 122-123
Parking 66-67, 71, 99, 198, 200
Pathology 78-79, 212, 218, 220
Peer Review 130
Personality
   match 59, 105, 113
   obsessive compulsive 64, 80
   profile 88
   traits 12, 118, 221
Pets 108
Phototherapy 184
Physical 51
   clutter 149
   fitness 39, 180
   health 22
   movement 187-188
   tension 144

Physiology and Biophysics 74-75
Positive intention 151-152, 173
Post Traumatic Stress 161
Pressure, deep 11
Preventative 132, 144
Primary School 28, 34, 57, 145
Private practice 146
Psychiatry 79-81, 88, 118, 122, 133, 217, 219
    Child and Adolescent 105, 220-221
    Training 100-103, 127-130

Q
Qi Gong 23, 189-190, 195
Questions, job interview 99, 101-102

R
Reflection, self 153
Rehabilitate 171
Relationships 40, 47-48, 52-53, 61, 166, 170
    Romantic 52, 68

Relaxation 108, 178, 189
Religion 45
Religious 14-15, 45, 195
Registrar 101
Researcher 124-126
Resilience 99, 164
Resume, also see Curriculum Vitae 126
Rituals 13-15, 45, 155, 159, 195
Resident Medical Officer 100
Role models 16, 18
Routines 155, 204, 215

S
Scapegoat 133
School
    choice 40
    primary 28, 37, 57, 145
    high 51, 54, 145
    medical 62, 65, 89-90
Screening 109
Self-care 148, 221
Self-esteem 42, 44, 105, 129, 144, 209

Sensitivity 3
  Noise 113
Sensory 11, 24-26, 28, 39-43, 48, 90, 92, 94, 146, 148-149, 184, 200
  thermometer 146
Sexual identity 54
Sexuality, including asexuality 53-54, 60, 96
Shift work 100
Sixth sense 59
Sleep
  consistent 112, 176
  diary 175
  hygiene 176, 182
  hypnosis 111, 177
  restoration and regeneration 174-177
  tablets 168
  tracking 187
Social skills 140-142
Social Scientist 72, 79, 212
Solitude 50, 54, 57, 68, 141
Special consideration 62, 89, 113

Special interests 27, 58, 98, 101, 116, 207
  antidote 44
  joint 68, 92
Specialties 1, 220-221
Spiritual, spirituality 15, 45, 128, 202
Stereotype 16, 204, 217
Stigma 101, 123, 155, 165
Strengths 92, 146, 221
  autism 98, 200
  leadership and management 109
  organizational 121
Stress 3, 39, 43, 113, 132, 144, 186
  action plan 95
  antidote 44
  management 41, 178-179
  signs 94-95, 99
Sugar 46, 158, 179, 182
Subspecialties 220
Suicidal 45, 160
Suicide 132, 221
  attacks 159

risk 160
Sunshine 183-185
Supervision 143, 154
Support 68, 102, 119, 160, 207-208, 222
    family 79
    group 38, 60, 92
    social 165

T
Tai Chi 23
Talents 101, 109, 113, 221
Team 3, 79, 107-108
    cohesion 114
    dynamics 107, 118
    meetings 114, 130
    multidisciplinary 101, 117
Teamwork 117, 120-121
Teased, Teasing 28, 38, 143
Technology 58, 146, 153
Telemedicine 129
Therapy 104-105, 129, 154, 162
    cognitive behavioural 111
Thinking 122, 159, 173, 179

black and white 71, 81, 119, 131, 173, 219
    depressive 151
    obsessive 155, 188, 195, 199
Tics 156
Tourette's Syndrome 96
Transformation 7, 111, 155, 173
Trauma 100, 190
Trust 42, 89
Tutorials 82

U
Universal Halo Effect 112
University 62, 65-66, 211-213
    recreation centre 69
    support group 92

V
Victim mindset 165

W
Ward rounds 82
Workplace 126-127
    accommodation 113

bullying 99, 129

clutter 147

disclosure 107

employment processes 108

interviews 88

politics 127

Printed in Great Britain
by Amazon